OSPREY COMBAT AIRCRAFT • 57

AH-64 APACHE
UNITS OF OPERATIONS
ENDURING FREEDOM
AND *IRAQI FREEDOM*

SERIES EDITOR: TONY HOLMES

OSPREY COMBAT AIRCRAFT • 57

AH-64 APACHE UNITS OF OPERATIONS
ENDURING FREEDOM AND *IRAQI FREEDOM*

JONATHAN BERNSTEIN

OSPREY
PUBLISHING

First published in Great Britain in 2005 by Osprey Publishing,
Midland House, West Way, Botley, Oxford OX2 0PH, UK
44-02 23rd St, Suite 219, Long Island City, NY 11101, USA
E-mail: info@ospreypublishing.com

Transferred to digital print on demand 2010

First published 2005
1st impression 2005

Printed and bound by PrintOnDemand-Worldwide.com, Peterborough, UK

A CIP catalogue record for this book is available from the British Library

ISBN: 978 1 84176 848 9

Edited by Tony Holmes
Page design by Tony Truscott
Cover Artwork by Mark Postlethwaite
Aircraft Profiles by Jim Laurier
Scale Drawings by Mark Styling
Index by Alan Thatcher
Originated by PPS Grasmere Ltd, Leeds, UK

Dedication

I wish to dedicate this book to CW3 Wesley 'Chuck' Fortenberry and CW2 Lawrence 'Shane' Colton from C Company, 1-227th
Attack Helicopter Battalion, CW4 Patrick D Leach and 1Lt Andrew C Shields from the 1-151st Aviation, South Carolina National
Guard, CW2 Nick DiMona and WO1 Bill Loffer from C Company, 1-3 Aviation, 3rd Infantry Division, and Capt Joseph F Lusk of 3-3
Aviation.
All seven Apache aviators gave their lives in the service of their country

Acknowledgements

The author would like to thank the numerous contributors to this book, specifically CW4 Zac Noble, CW2 John Rawls, Capts Joel
Magsig, Rogelio Garcia, Tom Potter and John Tucker, CW3 Rob Purdy, CW5 Jack Dalton, 1Sgt Rick Szlachta, Spc Antonio Allah,
Frank and John Musick, Scott Brown, Erick Swanberg and numerous others. Also, I would like to thank the cadre at TTU AROTC
(Lt Col James Skidmore, Capt Steven Dortch and MSgt Jon DeCavele), who have pushed me hard to get to where I can finally join the
ranks of outstanding men and women chronicled in this book. Thank you also to my family and friends, as well as to my fiancée Katie.

The editor would like to thank Maj David Rude, who wrote the 'Vipers'' War chapter. Thank you also to *Army Magazine* for allowing
Osprey to reproduce parts of Maj Rude's OIF article, which was originally published in this journal in July 2003.

Front cover

**AH-64D 99-5118 of 1-3 ATKHB's C Company 'Outcasts', piloted by CW3 Rob Purdy and CW2 Nick DiMona, flew an urgent
medevac escort mission on 31 March 2003. Having just returned from a combat sortie, Purdy and DiMona were shutting
down their Apache when their relief took off in 99-5104, lost visibility in the swirling sand and crashed. Purdy and DiMona
ran to the wrecked Apache and pulled its shaken, but relatively unharmed, crew (CW3 Cathy Jarrell and CW2 Mike Carman)
to safety. The two then returned to their aircraft and took off, escorting a 3rd Infantry Division medevac UH-60 to Nasiriyah.
Five wounded (three Americans and two Iraqis) were duly recovered and brought to safety. CW2 DiMona, who flew in every
battalion combat mission in OIF, was subsequently killed, along with fellow OIF veteran WO1 William Loffer, on 22 June 2004
in an AH-64D crash near Fort Stewart, Georgia (*Cover artwork by Mark Postlethwaite*)**

FOR A CATALOGUE OF ALL BOOKS PUBLISHED BY
OSPREY MILITARY AND AVIATION PLEASE CONTACT:

Osprey Direct, c/o Random House Distribution Center,
400 Hahn Road, Westminster, MD 21157
Email: uscustomerservice@ospreypublishing.com

Osprey Direct, The Book Service Ltd, Distribution Centre,
Colchester Road, Frating Green, Colchester, Essex, CO7 7DW
Email: customerservice@ospreypublishing.com

www.ospreypublishing.com

CONTENTS

OPERATIONAL HISTORY

The success of the US Army's AH-1 Cobra during the 1972 battle of An Loc in South Vietnam revolutionised army doctrine regarding the use of attack helicopters (see *Osprey Combat Aircraft 41 – US Army AH-1 Cobra Units in Vietnam* for details). The Cobra's victory against North Vietnamese armour validated the nascent theory that the best anti-tank platform was no longer another tank – it was an attack helicopter. This, along with the advent of the TOW (Tube-launched, Optically-tracked, Wire-guided) missile, proved the value of an airborne anti-tank weapons system. By the late 1970s, the two had been combined into a single platform in the form of the AH-1Q, which was at the heart of the US Army's anti-armor strategy as part of the NATO force in Cold War Europe. Yet by this time the Cobra was over ten years old.

Announced in August 1972 as an AH-1 replacement, the US Army's Advanced Attack Helicopter competition put forth the requirement for a dedicated anti-armour helicopter, mounting a powerful gun, missile and rocket armament. The helicopter also had to be capable of withstanding direct hits from 23 mm anti-aircraft fire. Focusing on the potential Soviet threat in Europe, this new machine would be the equalising factor, should communist armoured divisions ever attack Western Europe through the Fulda Gap in eastern Germany.

The Hughes YAH-64 was chosen for production as the Army's primary anti-armour helicopter in 1977 after beating off rival designs from Bell, Lockheed and Boeing. Production commenced in late 1982, and the 7th Battalion, 17th Cavalry Brigade, based at Fort Hood, Texas, accepted the first examples to attain frontline service in April 1986.

The new helicopter was built around a nose-mounted sensor turret, housing an ANS-170 Target Acquisition and Designation Sight (TADS)

The world's first dedicated attack helicopter, the Bell AH-1 Cobra saw over three decades of service with the US Army. This particular example is an AH-1S used by the massive US Army Training Center (part of US Army Training And Doctrine Command) at Fort Rucker, Alabama, in the 1980s. The Cobra had won its battle spurs in Vietnam between 1967 and 1973, with the battle of An Loc in 1972 proving that the ideal platform for killing tanks was the attack helicopter. Having ushered in a new age for Army attack aviation, the last Cobras were retired from frontline US Army service in 1999, although examples lingered on with the Army National Guard for another three years (*Mike Verier*)

in the lower turret and an AAS-11 Pilot's Night Vision Sensor (PNVS) mounted above. The TADS/PNVS turret is at the heart of the Apache's sensor suite, and it allows the helicopter to operate in virtually any weather. The TADS turret includes a FLIR sensor on the right side and laser designator on the left.

One of the AH-64's more remarkable advances in technology from previous attack helicopters is the flight crew's Integrated Helmet And Display Sighting System (IHADSS). This helmet-mounted device allows pilots to simply look at their intended target, and the slaved sensor turrets and chin-mounted M230 30 mm chain gun will follow, dramatically improving the helicopter's first-shot kill capability.

COMBAT DEBUT

As a reaction to escalating violence in Panama and direct provocation by its leader, President Manuel Noriega, the US military launched Operation *Just Cause* on 19 December 1989 to capture the country's leader and restore order to the Central American nation. Eleven Apaches of the 1st Battalion, 82nd Aviation Regiment (operating as Task Force *Wolf*) self-deployed from Fort Bragg, North Carolina, the helicopters flying well over 1000 miles to engage targets in support of Task Force *Bayonet*. Once in Panama, the Apaches operated alongside US Army OH-58Cs and AH-1Es until the ceasefire of 9 January 1990. Aside from the AH-64 making its combat debut, *Just Cause* also saw NVGs and Hellfire missiles employed by the Army for the first time.

According to the operation's overall commander, Gen Stiner, the Apaches were extremely precise with their targeting. He stated that 'You could fire that Hellfire missile through a window from four miles away at night', which was exactly what the AH-64s did during the assault on President Noriega's headquarters. The Apaches were involved in some of the heaviest fighting of the operation during their 247 combat hours, and although most sustained minor damage from small arms fire (one was hit 23 times), the Apache was able to absorb punishment and remain in the fight as advertised, thus accomplishing all of its assigned missions.

One year after operations in Panama, nearly half of the Army's Apache force was deployed to Saudi Arabia in response to Iraq's August 1990 invasion of neighboring Kuwait. In all, 273 AH-64As were positioned

YAH-64 prototype AV-02 was the first test example to be flown on 30 September 1975. No TADS/PNVS nose turret has yet been fitted, and the helicopter features the original T-tail, reduced cheek fairings and small engines (*Boeing*)

A close-up view of the Lockheed Martin (formerly Martin Marietta) TADS/PNVS sensor turret. The upper turret houses the Pilots Night Vision System and functions independently of the lower turret. The Target Acquisition/Designation Sight system is the larger lower turret. The turret's FLIR sensors are hidden behind the window on the left, these allowing the Apache's crew to see thermal images at night and in bad weather, while the housing on the right contains the turret's Laser Spot Tracker, Laser designator/range finder and an electro-optical TV camera system (*Robert Hewson*)

Operation *Desert Storm* saw the first widespread combat use of the AH-64A in its designated role as a deep attack tank hunter. This particular machine was from the 2nd Battalion, 229th Aviation Regiment, which deployed from Illesheim, Germany, in January 1991. The conflict saw Apaches working in tandem with OH-58A/C Kiowa scout helicopters as hunter-killer teams in much the same way as similar formations had operated in Vietnam 20 years earlier (*Yves Debay*)

along the Saudi frontier in the following months. Initial difficulties adapting the Apache to the desert environment caused some concern for military planners, as well as a great deal of consternation to crews and maintenance personnel. The talc-fine sand synonymous with this region tended to get inside the helicopter itself, causing serious problems with auxiliary power units and components of the ever-essential air-conditioning systems.

At 0056 hrs on 17 January 1991 – the opening night of Operation *Desert Storm* – nine Apaches from the 1st Battalion, 101st Aviation Regiment, escorting two USAF MH-53Js and one UH-60, played a key role in eliminating Iraqi early warning radar stations near the border with Saudi Arabia, which in turn opened the air corridor to Baghdad. Moving at low altitude and low speed, Lt Col Dick Cody's Task Force *Normandy* snuck in under the targeted Iraqi radars and fired the first shots of the campaign.

Throughout the rest of the brief war, Apaches worked primarily as they were intended to – as a stand-off tank-killing platform, utilising Hellfire missiles, rockets and 30 mm cannon fire to eliminate conventional armoured forces. Apaches were able to destroy a number of Iraqi armoured units before the ground invasion even began. When it was launched, on 24 February 1991 (G-Day), Apaches provided close air support to advancing Coalition forces, destroying armoured and soft-skinned vehicles wherever they were found. Overall, AH-64s flew nearly 19,000 hours, with a mission readiness rate of over 90 per cent – a figure much higher than normal. Apache units claimed more than 500 armoured vehicles destroyed and, incredibly, several hundred Iraqi soldiers captured.

Throughout *Desert Storm*, only one AH-64 was brought down, when it was hit by a rocket-propelled grenade (RPG) in the right engine. The crew carried out an emergency forced landing and were quickly recovered by the second Apache in their fire team, which flew them to safety clinging to the second AH-64's stub wings!

UPGRADES AND IMPROVEMENTS

Lessons learned from *Desert Storm* were rapidly integrated into planned upgrades for the Apache force. Initially, the Army was to fund the modification of 264 A-models into AH-64Bs, the 'new' helicopters featuring secure radios, GPS navigation systems and improved rotor blades. GPS, while in existence during *Desert Storm*, had not yet been fitted to frontline Apaches. Because of this, the AH-64s of Task Force *Normandy* had had to follow GPS-equipped USAF MH-53J *Pave Low* helicopters of the 1st Special Operations Wing to their various release points before striking Iraqi radars.

Although funding for the upgrades would be cancelled in 1992, most of these systems would eventually be included in active AH-64A airframes from 1994 onwards as part of the force modernisation programme for the Apache fleet as it neared its second decade of frontline service. The AH-64B designation was never officially adopted, the Army preferring instead to proceed with the AH-64C/D subtypes.

The D-model was designed to bring the Apache into the digital era. New avionics would enable crews to share secure information via data-link, assign targets and gain a real-time picture of the battlefield. A complete 'glass cockpit' would give them all the necessary information they required on large, colour multifunction displays (MFDs) on the pilot's and co-pilot/gunner's panels. Along with increased situational awareness, the APG-78 millimetre-wave radar mounted atop the rotor mast could simultaneously track hundreds of targets and prioritise the 16 most threatening. From there, information could be passed via secure data-link to other Apaches in the fire team and the threats eliminated.

McDonnell Douglas' AH-64D Longbow Apache demonstrator is seen carrying a full weapons load of 16 Hellfire missiles during a press demonstration in the mid-1990s. By 1997 this aircraft was wearing Boeing titling (*Ted Carlson*)

The AH-64C was to have been a radarless D-model that retained the latter's avionics and full capabilities. Both types would enter initial production in 1995 as the AH-64D (the AH-64C designation was dropped in 1993), those with radars being unofficially referred to as DWI, and those without DWO – officially, the two versions were the AH-64D Apache (no radar) and the AH-64D Longbow Apache (with radar). Production figures would be roughly three-to-one in favour of aircraft without the radar system.

The first 24 AH-64Ds were delivered to the US Army in the spring of 1997. After training instructors on the new aircraft, the Army selected the 1st Battalion, 227th Attack Helicopter Regiment to be the first operational Longbow Apache unit. After eight months of training at Fort Hood as part of the 21st Cavalry Group, the 1st Cavalry Division's 1-227th Aviation Battalion (AVN) was declared fully operational on 19 November 1998.

Despite the advent of the AH-64D, the original AH-64A continued to soldier on alongside its more technologically advanced younger brother. Alpha model upgrades, including an ECM suite, laser detectors and wire strike kits, along with the D-model's more powerful General Electric T700-GE-701C engines, added significantly to the older AH-64A's survivability and lethality in a hostile environment. At the turn of the millennium, the Apache in either form was the most capable and lethal attack helicopter in frontline service anywhere in the world.

WAR

The events of 11 September 2001 shocked the world. The terrorist attacks on the World Trade Center in New York City and the Pentagon in Washington, DC killed over 3000 American and foreign citizens, and set the United States on the path to war. It soon became obvious that Osama bin Laden's al-Qaeda terrorist group had carried out these attacks, undertaken by individuals trained in camps located in Afghanistan. The US government immediately demanded that the Taleban regime, then in power in Afghanistan, hand over bin Laden and his followers or face military action.

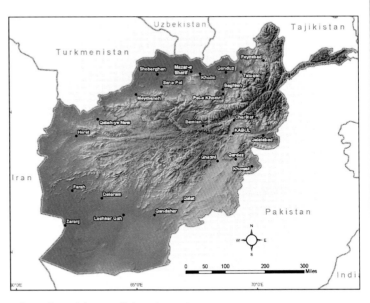

Terrain map of Afghanistan

Two fire teams of AH-64As from 3-101 AVN and a team of CH-47s from the 159th Aviation Brigade prepare to launch from Bagram as part of a combat air assault into the mountains of Afghanistan in 2002 (*US Army*)

Having received no positive response from the Taleban mullahs ruling Afghanistan, the US government duly gave the order for carrier-based US warplanes to go into action on 7 October 2001 (just 26 days after the 11 September attacks), strike aircraft attacking targets across the country as part of Operation *Enduring Freedom* (OEF). Air power played a crucial role from the war's outset, effectively neutralising the Taleban's entire command and control network, while at the same time attempting to preserve what little infrastructure the country had.

On the ground, small teams of Special Operations Forces (SOF) operated with Northern Alliance rebels against the Taleban from the beginning of the campaign, but it would be more than three months before US Army infantry units could be brought in to take the fight to al Qaeda. In early December the 3rd Ranger Battalion parachuted into Kandahar, seizing and securing the airport so that the first large ground units could begin arriving by USAF transports. A massive airlift operation then began, bringing in new troops and equipment to engage the Taleban and al-Qaeda forces directly.

The first elements of the 10th Mountain Division arrived in-theatre in December 2001, and they were followed shortly thereafter by the 3rd Brigade, 101st Airborne Division in January 2002. The latter brought with it the first land-based attack helicopter assets allocated to OEF, the 3rd Battalion, 101st Aviation Regiment deploying with 18 AH-64As during the last week of January. The unit immediately made its presence known.

One of the first combat missions flown was to cover a SOF 'snatch and grab' raid, where a joint force of US Navy SEALS (Sea, Air and Land Special operations team) and Danish Commandoes were tasked with the capture of Mullah Khairullah Kahirkhawa, the governor of Herat and a key Taleban figure. A Predator Unmanned Aerial Vehicle (UAV) had been monitoring activity in Paktia province, searching for 'wanted personalities', when it detected the mullah leaving a safehouse in a village near the Pakistan–Afghan border. Piling into the back of a USAF MH-53, the SEALS and Danish Commandoes were airborne in less than 15 minutes, while a single Apache from the 3-101 AVN fell in as their transport's armed escort. The mission went flawlessly, and the SOF troops quickly apprehended Kahirkhawa. Within 90 minutes of the first warning order, the Joint Forces team was back at Camp Rhino (the main US base in the region, located some 60 miles south-west of Kandahar) with the prisoner.

OPERATION *ANACONDA*

Initial contact with enemy forces was sporadic until the first week of March 2002, when US and Northern Alliance troops initiated Operation *Anaconda* in the Shah-i-Kot valley in north-eastern Afghanistan. This offensive took the form of a simple 'hammer-and-anvil' assault, with Task Force *Rakkasan* (comprised of the 1st and 2nd Battalions, 187th Infantry, as well as the 1st Battalion, 87th Mountain Infantry) taking up blocking positions along the valley. From here they would engage Taleban troops and al-Qaeda fighters flushed out by Commander Ziahuddin's Northern Alliance forces as they pushed along the valley floor.

The US element of the operation was led by Col Frank Wiercinski, (call-sign 'RAK 6'), and his intent was simple:

A CH-47D Chinook from the 101st Airborne Division's 159th Aviation Brigade stands ready to load troops from Task Force *Rakkasan* at Kandahar air base in preparation for Operation *Anaconda*. A 'Killer Spade' AH-64A from A Company, 3-101 AVN is already airborne, providing overhead security for the airport (*US Army*)

This Concept of Operations map for Operation *Anaconda* was released to the media soon after the offensive had commenced on 2 March 2002. It shows the various insertion points, avenues of approach and blocking positions that Col Frank Wiercinski intended TF *Rakkasan* to occupy during *Anaconda* (*US Army*)

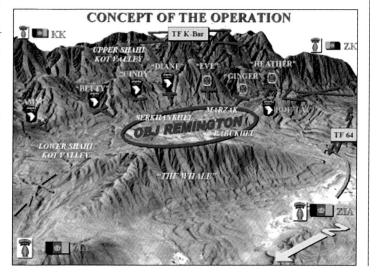

CONCEPT OF THE OPERATION

'Task Force *Rakkasan* is to air assault into Area of Operations (AO) "Eagle" [Shah-i-kot valley] to block an al-Qaeda withdrawal from Objective Remington in order to enable the combat operation of Commander Ziahuddin's Afghan force. On order, Task Force *Rakkasan* will assist Afghan forces to block al-Qaeda escape routes into Pakistan to complete the destruction of the enemy in AO "Eagle".'

Once the mission was accomplished, the task force was to redeploy back to Kandahar for future operations. The operation was intended to last three days, but the realities of combat would soon change that.

Since Task Force *Rakkasan* (and its two subordinate task forces *Summit* and *Raider*) was staging from Kandahar, several hundred miles south-west of the intended AO, a Forward Operating Base (FOB) had to be established at Bagram airfield, north of the city of Gardez, in order to sustain operations for at least a week. From there, a Forward Arming and Refuelling Point (FARP, call-sign 'Texaco') would be established closer to the AO in order to minimise the turnaround time between sorties, and allow a staging area for the battalion Quick Reaction Force (QRF).

For the operation, the 'Killer Spades' of A Company, 3-101 AVN would be flying cover for the combat air assault, as well as providing a Close Combat Attack (CCA) umbrella over friendly troops on the ground. The company's six Apaches were the airborne eyes of the task force, as well as their mobile artillery – a role that would prove crucial during the combat operations that followed.

D-DAY – 2 MARCH 2002

By 0430 hrs on 2 March, the two 'Killer Spade' teams were already airborne. USAF F-15Es from the 4th Fighter Wing had prepped caves near the intended landing zones (LZs) with 2000-lb laser-guided bombs, and B-1Bs had hit targets along the 'Whale' – a ridgeline that formed the western border of the Shah-i-Kot.

Although the 'Killer Spades' had intended to launch the operation as an entire eight-ship company, two Apaches had remained in Kandahar, where the 101st's Third Brigade was headquartered. Of the remainder, the lead team was minus one AH-64 after it had developed a hydraulic leak from its M230 30 mm Chain Gun, leaving CW3 Bob Carr to remain behind while his Apache was repaired.

The Apache air mission commander, Capt Bill Ryan (call-sign 'Killer Spade 06'), had assigned his company's two teams to cover the two main LZs during the insertion, and to then provide Close Combat Attack support to those units once they were in contact.

CW3 Rich Chenault led the first team of two aircraft into the northern end of the Shah-i-Kot valley to survey the intended LZs before the lift helicopters arrived. Detecting

WO1 Brian Roush preflights an A Company, 3-101 AVN AH-64A at Bagram airfield in March 2002. Note that the helicopter has a single 230-gallon auxiliary fuel tank on its inner left stub wing pylon in place of a Hellfire launcher. This is a typical configuration for Apaches assigned to OEF (*US Army*)

no movement either in or near the designated areas, or around the village of Serkhanel, he radioed the code-word 'Ice' to confirm that the LZ was clear. The company's other fire team surveyed similar LZs around Blocking Positions (BPs) 'Ginger' and 'Heather', which were to the south where Task Force *Summit*'s 87th Infantry (part of the 10th Mountain Division) was to land.

A co-pilot/gunner's view of the approaches to the Shah-i-Kot valley in early March 2002. Note the stowed PNVS turret visible through the windscreen (*US Army*)

Even before the air assault began, the success of the operation was already in jeopardy, however. Commander Ziahuddin's forces had met fierce resistance, and some were pinned down by minefields and mortar fire, while others were in full retreat. According to Col Wiercinski, at that point Task Force *Rakkasan* became the operation's main effort.

CW3 Jim Hardy's team was to the south, observing the intended LZs for the 10th Mountain Division's Chinooks. Arriving over LZs 'Eve', 'Heather' and 'Ginger' ahead of the inbound troop-carriers, Hardy made an initial pass over what seemed to be yet another quiet area. However, when he banked around in order to make a second pass, it immediately became obvious that the enemy was awaiting the helicopters' arrival. Small-arms fire began impacting his Apache, which Hardy later described as feeling like he was 'running over speed bumps'. The TADS/PNVS systems cut out a second later, having been damaged by a well-aimed RPG round. This left Hardy and his front seater, CW2 Stan Pebsworth, without a targeting system or weapons to shoot.

Meanwhile, having been informed of the resistance being encountered by Commander Ziahuddin's retreating forces in the mouth of the Shah-i-Kot valley, CW3 Chenault's fire team reacted quickly to their withdrawal by leaving their orbit over the northern LZs in order to assist the embattled Afghans and SOF soldiers pinned down by mortar fire. By then, SOF advisor CW2 Stanley Harriman had already been killed by incoming mortar fire, and the situation on the ground was becoming desperate.

After receiving a positive identification on the location of an enemy mortar team, both Chenault and CW3 Hurley rolled in and fired several pairs of rockets at the offending site. After their second pass the mortar fire ceased. Moving rapidly to the next target, Chenault coordinated directly with SOF teams on the ground to eliminate the most pressing threats.

A second mortar site on the 'Whale' was soon located, but Chenault and Hurley experienced difficulty in neutralising it. Having to get in close in order to bring their weapons to bear, the two Apache pilots established a racetrack pattern over the target and took it in turns to make firing passes with rockets and 30 mm cannon. While engaging a squad-sized element with his cannon, Hurley's Apache was hit by an RPG in the left wing, blowing off three of his Hellfire missiles and spraying his outboard rocket pod with shrapnel. Small-arms fire then perforated the Apache,

Top and above
These photograph reveal the extent of the damage sustained by CW3 Keith Hurley's Apache during the initial phase of Operation *Anaconda*. The impact of the RPG round on the port-side Hellfire launcher is clearly visible. Only one of the four missiles remained on the rack, although this was also damaged, rendering it unusable (*US Army*)

hitting the oil reservoir in the process. Immediately taking evasive action, Hurley flew over the 'Whale' and out of radio range from the remainder of his fire team. Although a few tense moments ensued when Chenault could not contact Hurley on the radio, the latter's break over the 'Whale' was an extremely fortuitous move that allowed him to contact elements of the southern fire team and join up with Jim Hardy.

The 10th Mountain Division's sector had immediately turned into an unforgiving battleground when the Chinooks touched down at BP 'Ginger' to disgorge their troops. Fighting their way to secure positions, troops hastily established a perimeter and called for Apache support. CW4 Hardy was acting as an aerial observer for the remainder of his team at this point, visually acquiring targets while keeping his machine moving to avoid ground fire.

When Hardy heard that Hurley's machine had been hit and was losing oil, he and Pebsworth had their wingman join up with Chenault's team while they broke off and met the outbound Hurley in an effort to assess the extent of the damage inflicted to the latter's Apache. Warning lights were lit up all over Hurley's instrument panel, and after a quick radio conversation, Hardy told him that he needed to land immediately.

The makeshift fire team set down in a dry riverbed that was still in range of enemy positions and shut down both helicopters. Hurley's Apache had over a dozen bullet holes in it, aside from the RPG shrapnel damage. The transmission oil reservoir was dry, and the two Apaches still had more than 50 miles to travel to the FARP at Bagram. With al-Qaeda fighters in the area, waiting for a Quick Reaction Force to secure the stricken Apache was not an option.

If the helicopter was left behind, Hurley and his front-seater, WO1 Stew Content, would have to fly out strapped to the wings of Hardy's Apache – this was dangerous enough under peacetime conditions, and the thought of enemy fighters taking potshots at them from the ground soon saw Hurley and Content abandon this option. The crew also quickly ruled out destroying the damaged Apache to prevent it from being exploited by the enemy.

Grabbing the spare oil cans from the cargo bays on both machines, Hardy proceeded to fill the aircraft with as much fluid as it would take, while instructing Hurley to switch helicopters with him – a move that he reluctantly agreed to. The 30-minute flight to 'Texaco' FARP was tense, but the battered fire team made it safely. Hardy's gamble worked. By putting enough transmission fluid in the helicopter to keep the moving parts moderately lubricated, he was able to exploit the Apache's rugged design, which allowed the machine to fly for 30 minutes without oil before breaking down. The team landed at 'Texaco' with roughly four minutes to spare.

A short time later, the remaining three Apaches in the Shah-i-Kot were forced to pull back to the FARP to refit after running low on fuel and ammunition. All had taken several hits, and Chenault's was the only one able to continue the fight. 3-101 AVN groundcrews immediately got to work repairing the damaged helicopters, and by the time Chenault's AH-64 had been refuelled and rearmed, CW3 Carr's Apache was also deemed fit enough to head back into the valley.

RAK 6 – CP UNDER ATTACK

Once the infantry task forces had been inserted, Col Wiercinski's command team moved into the valley to set up their combat command post (CP) to manage the battle. Wiercinski, circling above in a command and control EH-60A Fix 2B (a second Blackhawk carried more CP personnel), felt it was necessary to get closer to the action, so he deployed his CP team into a small LZ near BP 'Ginger'. During the helicopters' approach to insert the command team, they started taking small-arms and RPG fire, which intensified as the element set down individually to deposit the command post unit. Pinned down by enemy fire from the moment they were dropped off, the CP team was nevertheless able to get to cover and begin returning fire.

By this time, Chenault's new fire team, with Carr leading, had returned to the Shah-i-Kot to look for targets. Notified that the Task Force CP was under fire, Carr and Chenault passed over the site to assess the situation. Without proper ID on the target, it would be impossible to engage the enemy without putting the CP, and thus the whole operation, in jeopardy. Col Wiercinski responded by marking his unit's position with an aerial identification panel, and once Carr's team verified the orange colour, they rolled in on the attack. With attention focused on the inbound Apaches, the fire on Wiercinski's CP eased a little, enabling them to get to better cover.

Carr and Chenault each made several passes, facing small-arms, machine-gun and RPG fire as they attacked. Having never been trained for 'running fire' (firing while diving on the target), Carr conducted a trial pass and found that he was able to employ his 30 mm cannon with great effect on several clusters of fighters that had fired RPGs at both his and Chenault's helicopters.

The Apache training programme had trained pilots in hover fire and nap-of-the-earth flying in order to maximise the helicopter's tank-killing abilities. However, in a close-in fight supporting troops on the ground, those tactics exposed the Apache to intense ground fire, ruling out any attempt at hover-firing.

After numerous passes over the target area, the enemy forces surrounding the CP had been sufficiently suppressed to allow the Apache team to be released to answer the many calls coming in from US infantry task forces requesting fire support. Moving further down the valley, Carr and Chenault rolled in to hit targets around BP 'Ginger', firing rockets and 30 mm cannon with devastating effect. Yet for every pass they made, the RPGs kept coming up at them. On their final run, Chenault's Apache took a number of hits on the aircraft's right side, knocking out his night vision and targeting capabilities. The team was then ordered back to 'Texaco' to assess the damage.

Chenault's Apache, although damaged, could still shoot, so both his and Carr's machines were refuelled, rearmed and joined by a third Apache recently flown up from Kandahar by CW3 Sam Bennett. Upon taking off, they were immediately contacted by TF *Summit* at BP 'Ginger'. As they headed towards *Summit*'s position, the surrounding valley erupted in volleys of RPG fire, although somehow all the grenades missed their targets.

By now the sun was beginning to set, creating visual problems for the fire team, and limiting their avenues of approach to the target area. Once establishing the best route in – a ridgeline that had clear fields of fire down into the enemy positions – they made several passes, and each time the enemy fire intensified. During one pass, a shoulder-launched SAM was fired at Chenault's aircraft – later in the battle, US forces found examples of both Russian-made SA-7s and Chinese copies of this weapon, designated the HN-5. The ALQ-144 IR jammer mounted behind the helicopter's main rotor performed flawlessly, distracting the missile and sending it spiralling into the ground.

With the anti-aircraft fire showing no sign of abating, and with Chenault's night vision equipment out of commission, the team departed for the FARP after dusk. Arriving home in total darkness, the 'Killer Spade' Apaches were set upon by groundcrewmen, who made hasty repairs to the damaged helicopters. That night, the close support mission was left to USAF AC-130H Spectre gunships, with the three combat-capable AH-64s being sent back into action once again early the following morning.

The Apaches were reinforced 48 hours later when the remaining helicopters from 3-101 AVN arrived at Bagram from Kandahar and began flying missions around the clock in support of TF *Rakkasan*. The addition of a further 16 AH-64As significantly lessened the workload placed on the original cadre of 'Killer Spade' aviators, who had been going non-stop for 48 hours trying to keep their machines in the air so as to provide the best close-in support they could to friendly forces.

Initial intelligence analysis of the enemy situation in the Shah-i-Kot had convinced Army planners that they only needed to assign a single Apache company (eight helicopters, which in this case had initially been reduced to five due to mechanical maladies early on in the operation) to *Anaconda*. The reality of the situation on the ground soon proved that while USAF and Navy fast jets were ideal for attacking pinpoint areas like cave complexes with JDAM bombs, using those aircraft in the close support mission put friendly troops in harm's way.

This left the Apache as the only aerial support platform available in-theatre that had the ability to get in close enough to actually see the enemy positions, as well as sufficient firepower to then deal with them in close proximity to friendly troops.

This 3-101 AVN graffiti was photographed on a wall at Bagram airfield in 2002 (*1Sgt Rick Szlachta*)

The Hindu Kush mountain range which divides north-eastern Afghanistan and Pakistan reaches altitudes above 12,000 ft, severely hampering helicopter operations due to the thin atmosphere at that altitude. Fully loaded Blackhawks have had a very difficult time lifting troops and supplies in the thin air, so CH-47Ds have typically been utilised to insert and extract troops throughout OEF (*US Army*)

During the 16-day operation, TF *Rakkasan* aviation assets performed 14 combat air assaults, often under fire, without the loss of a single soldier. Of the 1411 troops inserted, all of them were accounted for and extracted. The Apache force, while initially hit hard, fought tenaciously, using ingenuity and innovation to engage al-Qaeda and Taleban positions, sometimes at ranges of less than 200 metres.

By the time the entire 3-101st Attack Helicopter Battalion (ATKHB) arrived to join the fight, A Company had been flying virtually non-stop for two full days with machines that had taken a severe pounding. Of the seven AH-64As that saw action at some stage during D-Day, all had taken many small-arms hits, at least two were hit by RPGs, and four were so badly damaged by dusk on 2 March that they could not return to combat right away. Indeed, the helicopters' 28 main rotor blades all had bullet holes in them, save one.

As is always the case in a wartime situation, the groundcrews worked miracles to get the 'Killer Spade' Apaches back into the fight, and by 4 March all but one had rejoined the battle.

Probably the most telling testament to the outstanding performance of A Company's crews and machines came from Task Force commander Col Wiercinski:

'I was just so impressed by its capability. I had never seen the Apache in combat before, although I've always trained with it. I am a firm believer right now that a brigade combat team commander needs his Apache battalion in an air assault division – its ability to protect us en route, its ability to set the conditions on the landing zones and then its close combat attack capability to take out fires.

'Artillery is a wonderful asset, but you need an observer, you need a sensor, and you've got the artillery as the shooter. An Apache can do all of that, and it is always moving.'

MEDEVAC ESCORT – AFSOC STYLE

The 3-101 AVN Apaches continued around-the-clock operations throughout March and April, although for the remainder of the unit's tour combat would not be as intense as it had been during *Anaconda*. The

'Eagle Attack' pilots were kept busy, nevertheless, flying anti-mortar patrols, responding to requests for air support and escorting medevac and air assault missions.

In early April, CW3 Rich Chenault and Capt Joe Herman responded to an urgent request to escort a USAF Special Operations Command MH-53M Pave Low IV that had been sent to rescue two critically wounded Coalition soldiers from the battlefield. 1Lt John Totty, who was one of the Pave Low aircraft commanders (and a former Apache Standardisation Instructor Pilot (SIP) before transferring to the Air Force), was to lead a flight of two MH-53s deep into hostile territory to attempt the rescue. However, on run-up, his wingman's helicopter went down with maintenance problems and it was unable to take off. Quickly requesting Apache support for the mission, Totty duly departed alone. He later recalled:

'At short notice, AH-64s were requested and immediately stepped in to provide my security en route. Our intended pick-up was a Northern Alliance soldier who had been shot four times in a gun battle that was still raging outside his safe house. We did our best to get to him as quickly as possible, using my radar to guide us through some terrible thunderstorms and rain which blocked our ingress to the target area.'

Working in near-zero visibility and horrible weather conditions, Chenault's team stayed in tight formation with 1Lt Totty's Pave Low helicopter, despite having minimal all-weather capability and no weather radar. By the time the helicopters had arrived on scene, the Northern Alliance unit had been surrounded by Taleban and al-Qaeda forces, so Chenault's team laid down suppressive cannon and rocket fire while the MH-53M Pave Low landed to pick up the wounded soldier. Totty continued:

'I just can't say enough about the Apache crews' total dedication that night. We would have launched as a singleton given the nature of the mission, but the outcome might have been different. Bottom line – we got to the guy and got him out. I had a surgeon on board my aircraft that operated on him en route, and we were able to get him stable enough to have him airlifted to a hospital in Germany.'

After returning to base, the Pave Low/Apache team was called upon an hour later to perform the same mission once again, with similar results.

Operations continued throughout April 2002, with 'Eagle Attack' Apaches supporting both SOF and 101st Airborne's 3rd Brigade. On the 11th, two A Company Apaches were returning from a night mission at a height of 150–200 ft when the pilot in the lead aircraft in the team radioed that he was going down. The circumstances are still unclear as to what caused the Apache to crash, but it did not seem to be ground fire. AH-64A 88-0209 came down roughly 40 miles north of Kandahar, the helicopter impacting the ground and

3-101 ATKHAB AH-64A 88-0209 suffered a catastrophic mechanical failure and crashed during a night mission on 11 April 2002. Amazingly, both pilots survived with recoverable injuries. The wreck is seen here just prior to it being blown up in place by SOF demolition experts (*Chinook-helicopter.com*)

then bouncing back into the air for 90 ft. It then hit the ground for a second, and final, time, sliding some 45 ft before coming to rest upright, seriously injuring both crewmen. The AH-64's right stub wing stores had been ripped from the wing, its undercarriage collapsed, tail boom severed and both engines and transmission displaced as a result of the impact.

The Apache in trail landed and quickly extracted the injured crewmen from the wreckage, the pilot and gunner securing them to the exterior of their helicopter and then taking off for a safer extraction point, where a medevac UH-60 could pick them up. Although both crewmen sustained compound fractures to their legs and broken jaws, and one suffered a compressed spine, they would eventually make full recoveries.

The following day, a mission was mounted by units of the 101st Aviation Brigade and Canadian infantry from the 3rd Battalion, Princess Patricia's Canadian Light Infantry Regiment to assess the crash site and determine whether 88-0209 could be saved. When the US salvage team and Canadian infantry platoon providing security reached the crash site, it was clear that there was no way the aircraft could be salvaged.

Its ordnance, strewn about the crash site, was duly gathered up and placed underneath the twisted fuselage, followed by nearly 200 lbs of plastic explosive. AH-64A 88-0209 was practically vapourised in the ensuing explosion, which threw pieces of the helicopter up to a mile from the crash site. When the demolition team subsequently returned to the site, there was nothing left but a smoking hole where the $15.94 million Apache had once been.

ESCORT, STABILISATION AND COUNTER-INSURGENCY

Although trained primarily for deep-attack anti-armor missions, the pilots of 3-101 AVN adapted quickly to their new environment in Afghanistan, using the Apache as a true multi-role attack helicopter, instead of simply an anti-armour weapons platform.

Since targets were primarily personnel, caves and light vehicles, 'Eagle Attack' pilots reduced Hellfire loads to just two missiles, preferring instead to carry full rocket pods and cannon ammunition. In some cases, Hellfires would be deleted on one wing in favour of a 230-gallon auxiliary fuel tank, while two missiles would be carried on the opposite wing, thereby compensating for some of the immense distances that were covered on most missions. These lighter combat loads also gave the Apache a greater ability to operate in the thin mountain air of eastern Afghanistan, where patrols were performed at altitudes that sometimes exceeded 12,000 ft.

Combat sorties continued through May and June, but against small pockets of Taleban and al-Qaeda resistance. The large-scale operations like *Anaconda* had ceased, leaving enemy forces scattered in disarray. When the battalion began winding down operations in early June 2002, members of its replacement battalion's advanced party began accompanying 'Eagle Attack' pilots on missions to familiarise themselves with the terrain, operations and types of sorties that they would fly upon the arrival of the remainder of their unit. Lessons learned by one battalion were quickly adopted into the Standard Operating Procedures of the next to ensure a fairly seamless transition.

ROTATION

Following the successes of 3-101 AVN in OEF, a second battalion of Apaches was sent to Afghanistan in June 2002. The 1st Battalion, 229th Attack Helicopter Regiment's advanced party flew several missions with 3-101 AVN fire teams in order to familiarise themselves both with the local terrain and the unit's new AO. While the 1-229th AHR was gearing up to begin operations from Kandahar, the 101st Airborne's 3rd Brigade was ordered home to Fort Campbell, Kentucky, to begin training with the rest of the division for upcoming operations elsewhere.

By mid-July the entire 1-229th had arrived in-country, and the regiment began operations in support of XVIII Airborne Corps as soon as its Apaches were reassembled. The 2nd Brigade Combat Team of the 82nd Airborne Division was also brought in by XVIII Airborne Corps at this time in order to replace US infantry assets being rotated out.

CW3 Zac Noble, SIP for 1-229th ATKHB's C Company, summed up the battalion's sentiments toward the deployment as follows:

'We were pleased to be a part of the force participating in Operation *Enduring Freedom*. After all, we were on a mission designed to retaliate against the terrorists who had attacked our nation. We were going to war for the first time since 1942 against an enemy who attacked our people on our soil. We were defending our nation in the purist sense.'

These two 'Blue Max' AH-64As are seen neatly packed aboard a USAF C-17 transport en route to Afghanistan in June 2002. The Air Force transport can carry two Apaches in its cargo hold, complete with crews and equipment. In 2003, a new blade-fold system was incorporated into Lot 7 AH-64Ds which eliminated the need to disassemble the rotor system. Because of this innovation, deployment time was shortened considerably, with landing to flight time reduced from hours to minutes (*1Sgt Rick Szlachta*)

An aerial view of Kandahar air base from the front seat of an AH-64. Chinooks, Blackhawks and Apaches are visible in this photograph. The tent city in the upper right hand corner of the shot is the pilot and groundcrew living area (*CW4 Zac Noble*)

Although CW3 Noble was part of C Company, 'Blue Max', he was attached to the 'Raiders' of B Company, 1-229 ATKHB for most of his time in Afghanistan.

OPERATION *MOUNTAIN SWEEP*

The first major operation conducted by XVIII Airborne Corps was a brigade-sized effort aimed at reducing the Taleban/al-Qaeda presence in the Pakistani border region. Seven infantry battalions moved into Paktia province, south-east of Bagram, on 18 August, including elements of the 3rd Ranger Battalion, 82nd Airborne, 10th Mountain Division, US, Dutch and Australian Special Operations Forces and Afghan militia. According to Col Roger King, Public Affairs Officer for XVIII Airborne Corps and Coalition Joint Task Force 180 (CJTF-180), 'The objective of *Mountain Sweep* was to find and destroy remaining al-Qaeda fighters in the area, search for weapons and usable intelligence data and project combat power into the region so as to deny the enemy sanctuary there.'

Two methods of insertion were used for the operation. The first units were combat air assaulted to their positions by CH-47s, while other assault forces moved by truck convoy, sweeping the area for signs of enemy activity, weapons caches and any possible intelligence material. The air assault portion of the operation relied on heliborne transport from elements of the 101st and 159th Aviation Brigades, as well as units from the 101st Airborne Division that had not yet rotated back to the US. They, in turn, depended on the 1-229th for combat escort and aerial fire support during troop offloading. Although enemy contact was infrequent, the 'Tigershark' pilots of the 1-229th played an essential role in the operation just by being there.

After Operation *Anaconda*, Taleban and al-Qaeda fighters gained a healthy respect for the Apache's ability to hunt them down day or night. When American helicopters were involved in operations, the enemy carefully chose when and where to fight. If AH-64s were in the area, more often than not no contact would be made.

Mountain Sweep was the battalion's first major operation, and according to Zac Noble, it was the largest offensive undertaken by the 'Tigersharks' in Afghanistan. Indeed, it was one of few missions where the entire battalion worked in unison:

'During that mission we provided escort and security coverage for the Chinooks of the 101st and 159th AVN and the Blackhawks of the 82nd AVN. Throughout the operation, we conducted close combat attack coverage for the 82nd Airborne Division, as well as for US and Australian SOF squads. The operation lasted for about eight days, and our unit flew around-the-clock close support for about six of them. We were working the high country along the Pakistani border, flying at altitudes up to 12,000 ft.

Hoisting the 'unofficial' colours of C Company are from, left to right, CW2 Scott McBride, Capt Pat Davis, CW2 Jerry Works and CW3 Zac Noble (*CW4 Zac Noble*)

The visualisation of an operation during the pre-mission briefing phase is often the key to its successful execution. Here, Kandahar-based C Company pilots from 1-229 AVN study a large terrain model of their Area of Operations during *Mountain Sweep* in August 2002 (*CW4 Zac Noble*)

A 'Blue Max' fire team covers the advance of 3/505th Paratroopers as they approach a stone fort during *Mountain Sweep* (*1Sgt Rick Szlachta*)

One of the numerous weapons caches seized by CTF-82 while 1-229 AVN was attached. At this particular site, over a million rounds of 7.62 mm ammunition and 100 + RPG rounds were confiscated (*1Sgt Rick Szlachta*)

I remember being in the helicopter for over ten hours each day, making many trips through the FARPs at Bagram and Fire Base "Chapman" [later to be moved to FB "Salerno"], near Khowst.'

The 1-229th Apaches escorted all five combat air assault insertions during the eight-day campaign, beginning with C Company, 3rd Battalion, 505th Parachute Infantry Regiment at LZ 'Beretta'. The 'Tigersharks' then stayed on station to provide overhead security for the ground elements, including the convoys that were slowly making their way through the valley.

At a press briefing held at the time, CJTF-180 spokesman Maj Gary Tallman stated:

'This was the first opportunity for the 82nd to project combat power in the theatre, and they did it in a professional manner. During the operation, 82nd paratroopers discovered five separate weapons caches and two caches of Taleban documents. The operation took place mainly around the villages of Dormat and Narizah, south of the cities of Khowst and Gardez. The troopers found a ZPU-23-2 towed artillery gun, two 82 mm mortars and ammunition, a recoilless rifle, rockets, rocket-propelled grenades, machines guns and thousands of small arms rounds.'

Elsewhere during the operation, further caches of documents were discovered that ultimately provided valuable intelligence. Aside from the weapons and documents that were seized, ten suspects were also captured and sent to Bagram airbase for interrogation.

The ground elements came under fire twice during the offensive, but with Apaches operating overhead, the engagements were short lived. The one major incident that affected the aviators of the 1-229th occurred on the first day of *Mountain Sweep*, and clearly displayed the unforgiving environment in which US forces were flying. CW3 Bill Sullivan and CW2 Jeff Bartlett were sitting in the alert Apache (88-0261) on QRF duty when the call for a medevac came in. The AH-64 duly escorted the medevac UH-60 to the pick-up point, but in the thin air, fully loaded with fuel and ammunition, the Apache became sluggish and unresponsive just as the UH-60 landed.

The helicopter went down close to the medevac pick-up and the Blackhawk's crew chief was able to pull the stunned crew from the wreckage. As with the crash of 88-0209 several months before, the helicopter literally rolled itself into a ball of twisted metal, but the crew compartment maintained its structural integrity and both Sullivan and Bartlett escaped with only minor injuries. It was simply a case of too little power available and too much power demanded from the machine.

Another contributory factor in this aircraft's demise is the possibility that it may not have been fitted with the newer General Electric T700-GE-701C engines, and therefore did not have the necessary power reserves available to maintain flight. The wreckage was subsequently picked over for salvageable components prior to being destroyed by the demolition experts from the 19th Special Forces Group (Reserve).

After *Mountain Sweep*, the 1-229th was divided between Bagram in the east and Kandahar in the south. The 'Stalkers' and 'Raiders' of A and B Companies remained at Bagram, while 'Blue Max' headed 350 miles south to stage from Kandahar. This splitting up of the battalion, although logistically bothersome, allowed for much greater coverage of the border region where the enemy combatants were known to have taken refuge.

ALAMO SWEEP

While regular patrolling of the AO continued into the early autumn of 2002, the next major operation for the 1-229th began in mid-September. This took the form of a series of exercises, the largest of which was *Alamo Sweep*, as well as Sensitive Site Exploitations (SSE) conducted in conjunction with Combined Task Force 82 (also referred to as Task Force *Panther*). This organisation, comprised of the 82nd Airborne's 2nd Brigade Combat Team and various SOF detachments, was air assaulted into the mountains near Khowst, in eastern Afghanistan.

The operation's intent was to utilise larger numbers of conventional troops to hunt down al-Qaeda and Taleban fugitives, instead of restricting such tasks to SOF squads only. Ultimately, this tactical change proved successful, although the actual methods of execution employed caused some contention between SOF and 82nd Airborne soldiers.

The 1-229th provided aerial security for the entire operation, having 'eyes-on' the advancing troops at all times. To augment this force, one fire team was kept on 24-hour QRF status. The battalion also provided Blackhawk medevac escort on several occasions during the six-week-long operation.

IN-COUNTRY TRAINING

While 1-229 ATKHB was conducting combat operations throughout its time in-country, on occasion the mission tempo allowed for further

AH-64s and 82nd Airborne infantry train for Sensitive Site Exploitation during Exercise *Alamo Sweep* (*1Sgt Rick Szlachta*)

C Company's standard armament package is clearly visible here – two Hellfire missiles and 30 high explosive rockets, with eight flechette rockets in the first four firing slots per launcher. Unseen is the 130-gallon belly tank that has replaced the 30 mm cannon magazine. Due to the immense distances travelled in the initial phases of the 229th's tenure in Afghanistan, it was determined that fuel was of greater importance than weaponry, so the ammunition for the 30 mm cannon was reduced to a mere 90 (instead of 1200) rounds (*1Sgt Rick Szlachta*)

Pilots from B Company load M151 10-lb HE rockets into the outboard M261 launcher. Groundcrews often had their hands full maintaining the unit's hard-worked helicopters, so pilots would gladly assist with the rearming of their aircraft (*CW4 Zac Noble*)

1Lt Steve Bouchard stands next to AH-64A 89-0260, which was the aircraft that he and CW3 Zac Noble were flying when it had an accessory transmission failure while they were escorting a VIP-laden UH-60 from Bagram to Kandahar (*CW4 Zac Noble*)

training sorties to be performed in order to keep aircrews proficient in certain flight profiles that they were not regularly flying in OEF.

Experimentation with varied weapons loads and fuel configurations was also carried out during the deployment, as the combat situation in Afghanistan dictated the carriage of anti-personnel-oriented ordnance over longer distances. As a result, many 'Tigersharks' Apaches adopted the standard weapons load of two 19-shot rocket pods, full ammunition for the 30 mm cannon and two Hellfire missiles in case a pinpoint target was encountered.

It is important to note the variation in the types of Hydra 70 rockets carried by the AH-64s. Since this weapons load was optimised for anti-personnel missions, the first four rockets to fire from both pods would be M255A1 flechettes, each carrying 1180 60-grain hardened steel 'nails', as the rounds are commonly referred to. Fitted with proximity fuses, each flechette would burst just above the ground, sending out a lethal circular cloud of high-speed 'nails' over a radius of 200 metres. The Apache's remaining 30 rockets would be a mix of the standard 10-lb M151 or M229 17-lb high explosive rounds.

The AH-64's range has always been an issue in OEF, and this was especially the case during the early missions flown in-country. Fuel was precious, and since setting down in the wilds of Afghanistan was extremely dangerous, there were times that additional gas was carried at the expense of ammunition. 1-229th pilots found that the addition of 130-gallon belly tanks in place of the cannon ammunition magazine enhanced mission range performance without degrading combat capability. The removal of the cannon magazine still allowed the carriage of 90 rounds of 30 mm ammunition, so the cannon was not rendered completely unusable.

In October 2002, the battalion was tasked with live-fire training with Hellfire missiles so as to maintain proficiency with this weapon. Because of the number of sorties being flown, and the extremely low number of Hellfires being shot in anger, commanders determined that it was necessary for 1-229 ATKHB pilots to get some practice in firing the weapon when they could. The training conducted at Kandahar also included live-fire artillery cooperation missions,

where Apaches acted as forward observers and laser designators for artillery fire-missions, thus further increasing the flexibility and lethality of the AH-64.

The 1-229th's Apaches also routinely provided armed escort for other Army aviation assets in-theatre. Occasionally, however, the escort became the escorted, as CW3 Zac Noble and 1Lt Steve Bouchard found out the hard way while covering a UH-60 carrying the 82nd Airborne's 3rd Brigade commander, Col James Huggins, from Bagram to Kandahar – a trip of 300-plus miles over hostile territory. This flight would usually last 3.5 hours, with a refueling stop at Firebase 'Orgun-E', in Paktia province, although on this particular occasion the mission seemed to last twice as long for the men involved.

Noble and Bouchard's AH-64A (89-0260) suffered a shaft-driven compressor failure about 100 nautical miles from Kandahar, which in turn caused an accessory transmission failure and the subsequent loss of all transmission fluid. The Apache crew had launched as a single-ship escort, meaning that they had only the brigade commander's UH-60 with them. Noble recalled:

'We immediately called the on-station AWACS and got an RAF Tornado on station to provide high coverage in the event we went down. We were about 70 minutes flying time from Kandahar when the failure happened. We would be over territory known to be hostile for the remainder of our flight.'

1Lt Bouchard flew the crippled Apache from the front seat while CW3 Noble coordinated with the AWACS, the British Tornado and the UH-60 that they were 'escorting', as well as the 'Blue Max' QRF waiting to launch from Kandahar in case they went down. Landing short of their objective was not an option, as according to intelligence reports, Taleban, al-Qaeda and Chechen fighters were abundant in the territory they were flying over. Noble continued:

'I had briefed Steve during our emergency that in the event we went down, he was to take both of our M4 Carbines and M9 pistols and defend us for as long as he could while I attempted to maintain radio contact with our air coverage in order to direct protective fire. When we finally landed at Kandahar our aircraft was completely out of trans-

Visor down, IHADSS (Integrated Helmet and Display Sight System) monocle extended and mike boom in front of his face, CW3 Zac Noble looks more like a character from a B-grade horror movie than Pilot in Command of AH-64A 89-0245 *DELIVERANCE* (*CW4 Zac Noble*)

AH-64A 89-0260 from B Company 'Raiders' was photographed soon after landing at Kandahar without any transmission fluid. The contents of the entire transmission fluid reservoir can be seen spread across the helicopter's tailboom (*CW4 Zac Noble*)

mission fluid. The "Blue Max" QRF pilots immediately came over to us with huge grins on their faces at seeing us safe. Knowing that a fellow "Blue Max" pilot was in trouble, they were more than prepared to take action to get both myself and 1Lt Bouchard back safely.'

SOF SUPPORT

The 'Tigersharks' also provided support for more clandestine missions carried out by US Special Operations Command (SOCOM) units during their deployment. Conducting operations with the Rangers and SOF teams was more intense, and contact was usually expected.

On 7 November, elements of the 3rd Ranger Battalion, operating in the mountainous border region near Pakistan, took fire from light machine guns dug in on a ridgeline above them. Realising it was virtually impossible to reach the position without being exposed, the Rangers called in Apache and A-10 strikes. The 'Stalkers' of A Company were on station, and they hit the target with rockets and 30 mm cannon fire, silencing the enemy guns.

Intelligence reports coming in on 24 November indicated the possibility of enemy forces massing for a large-scale attack on Coalition troops in the vicinity of Firebases 'Orgun-E', 'Shkin' and 'Lwara'. Convinced of the credibility of the reports, CTF-82 commander Maj Gen John Vines ordered an aviation QRF, consisting of four AH-64s and an EH-60 command and control aircraft, to move to 'Orgun-E' to provide immediate close combat attack, aerial security and airborne command and control capabilities to the area. The QRF was positioned at the FOB 24 hours later, and was standing by ready to launch for any area in the sector within 30 minutes' notice.

Early in the afternoon of 26 November, 'Lwara' firebase came under rocket attack from positions near the Pakistani border. The base commander at 'Lwara' immediately requested QRF assistance to locate and destroy the al-Qaeda rocket positions. A fire team comprised of two AH-64s, crewed by CW3 Glenn Osborne and 1Lt Bouchard (call-sign 'Raider 16') and CW2s Bobby Remington and Edward Schemper (call-sign 'Raider 12'), and an EH-60 (call-sign 'Jedi 09'), took off within 15 minutes of receiving the call and were on station over a SOF forward observer ('Playboy 16') eight minutes later.

'Playboy 16' relayed the suspected rocket location to the Command and Control Blackhawk, and from there the fire team was able to identify ten armed men moving away from the site towards the Pakistani border. 'Raider 12' was cleared by the EH-60 mission controller to cross the border in pursuit of these individuals, as they posed a definite threat. When the AH-64s approached, the al-Qaeda fighters attempted to flee. Meanwhile, the SOF personnel recovery team aboard the EH-60 requested to be inserted in order to investigate the rocket launch site.

Covering the insertion of the five-man team, the two AH-64s provided aerial security for both the EH-60 and the SOF team as they approached their objective. The suspects had attempted to escape into a small, multiple-building complex on the border, and they were soon intermingling with Pakistani troops manning the border guard post. The SOF team then called for an extraction and was exfilled within sight of the border post, covered by the two 'Raiders' AH-64As. A later review of the mission video taken by both Apaches clearly showed the suspects taking refuge across the border, and being supported in their endeavours by Pakistani troops. The 'Raiders' fire team then covered 'Jedi 09' as it headed back to 'Orgun-E', where the team debriefed.

Two nights later, 'Orgun-E' was again hit by rocket fire. The QRF – this time a three-Apache heavy team that included 'Raider 11', crewed by CW3 Zac Noble and CW2 David Thoresen – was sortied to locate and destroy the launch site. En route to the objective, the team took small-arms fire on three separate occasions. The Apache crews quickly found the new launch site, but failed to locate any suspects, so they were ordered by the ground QRF to conduct an investigative sweep of the area.

CW2 Dennis Jackson and CW3 Zac Noble conduct a crew mission briefing before heading out on a close combat attack sortie from Bagram (*CW4 Zac Noble*)

The final night of the operation was the most significant, yielding positive results that ensured 'Orgun-E' would be free from further rocket attacks. A SOF observation post ('Playboy 11') had detected several personnel acting suspiciously near the Pakistani border and had launched the QRF in response. Air mission commander CW3 Noble launched his heavy team, along with the Command and Control Blackhawk, in low visibility. En route, they again took well-aimed small-arms tracer fire, but no helicopters were hit.

After seeing the tracer fire, Noble called for the ground QRF ('Serpent 62') to launch from 'Orgun-E' in order to seize and exploit the rocket site – the 'Raider' fire team duly located five 107 mm rockets aimed towards 'Lwara' on a time-delay fuse. EOD specialists were called in to disarm the rockets and Noble then directed the ground QRF towards buildings into which the suspects had fled. 'Raiders 11' and '12' then engaged the building with 30 mm cannon fire, as well as providing overhead security for 'Serpent 62' as the ground team moved in to conduct an SSE. One suspect was captured at this point.

Meanwhile, 'Playboy 11' contacted 'Raider 16' and informed him that additional enemy troops were moving on foot approximately four kilometres to the south-west. Breaking from his overwatch position, 'Raider 16' directed the second ground QRF vehicle to this second site and then attacked with rockets and 30 mm cannon fire. Once the site was secured, 'Raider 16' moved to rejoin '11' and '12'. The team then received radio traffic that the base was under rocket attack from a different location. 'Raider 12' split off from the team and proceeded to the eight-digit grid coordinates that he had been given, where he quickly located the site and destroyed it.

The missions flown by 'Raiders' fire teams during this eight-day period effectively ended the daily rocket attacks on 'Orgun-E' through the neutralising of organised anti-US forces in the area.

By the time the 1st Battalion, 229th AVN left Afghanistan in late December 2002, it had flown more combat hours than any other Army

aviation unit since the war in Vietnam. The unit had averaged over 1200 combat hours per month as a battalion between the companies at Kandahar and Bagram. Battalion assets were spread thin in order to cover as much of the country as possible, but the areas in which most enemy contact occurred were focused equidistant from each base, allowing coordination between companies on some combat missions.

Almost all of the missions that were flown were performed by team-sized (two to six aircraft) formations so as to allow greater flexibility when responding to various combat situations. Hundreds of rockets and thousands of 30 mm cannon shells had been expended in support of friendly forces, the battalion having participated in six major campaigns that covered thousands of square miles. It had also maintained an extremely high mission readiness rate throughout its time in Afghanistan.

1-229 AVN's AH-64A 88-0202 *DEVIL'S DANCE* is 'hot refuelled' (the aircraft is not shut down) at the 'Orgun-E' FARP in August 2002 (*1Sgt Rick Szlachta*)

Back at its Kandahar base, AH-64A 88-0202 is prepped for its next OEF combat mission. Note how its *DEVIL'S DANCE* nickname appears here in white – this was later toned down to black, as shown in the photograph above (*1Sgt Rick Szlachta*)

REINFORCEMENTS

A s the 1st Battalion's operations wound down in Afghanistan, the 229th Attack Helicopter Regiment's 3rd Battalion was gearing up to replace it at Kandahar. The new battalion arrived in Afghanistan in early January 2003, and the 'Tigersharks' of the 1-229th ATKHB turned its AOR and its 16 AH-64As over to the 3rd Battalion. Now devoid of helicopters, the battalion was duly sent to Fort Hood to begin its conversion onto the AH-64D.

Like the 1-229th before it, the 3rd Battalion was immediately immersed in round-the-clock operations in a harsh and unforgiving environment, and had little time to adjust to combat operations. Its first exposure to the enemy came in mid-January 2003, when Apaches provided air cover for SOF and Afghan National Army (ANA) forces operating near the town of Spin Boldak.

Whilst in the process of clearing a compound, the soldiers had been attacked by small-arms and mortar fire around midday. The Coalition forces duly returned fire, killing one of their attackers, wounding a second and capturing a third, who confessed that a large contingent of Taleban and al-Qaeda fighters were hiding in the nearby Adi Ghar mountains. Their number was estimated at roughly company-size (120 to 150 men), which made it one of the largest enemy troop concentrations seen in quite some time.

Immediately, the 3-229th fire team designated to provide overwatch for the ground forces was despatched to reconnoitre the area. Approaching the Adi Ghar mountains, the two Apaches were fired on by small arms and withdrew, their initial mission complete. An 82nd Airborne Division QRF from the 505th Parachute Infantry Regiment (PIR) was then air assaulted into the area by CH-47, escorted by 'Flying Tigers' Apaches. Once the platoon-sized QRF was on the ground, the 229th aircraft took up overwatch positions for the advancing infantrymen, providing fire support as needed.

All the 'Tigersharks' battalion's aircraft were handed over to the 3rd Battalion, 229th Attack Helicopter Regiment when the 1-229th rotated to Fort Hood, Texas, in December 2002. This ex-1-229th machine is seen here taking on fuel at the 'Orgun-E' FARP (*1Sgt Rick Szlachta*)

Facing a large contingent of enemy forces, the ground commander also called in F-16 and AC-130 air strikes to complement the AH-64's close-in firing passes. Initial reports indicated that Coalition strikes killed an additional 18 enemy fighters. Firefights continued throughout the night, with Apaches and AC-130s flying a continuous umbrella over the 'All American' troops in contact. Additional reinforcements were air assaulted into the region towards the end of the first day of the battle, bringing the total Coalition forces engaged to roughly 250 soldiers.

As the operation progressed, US troops discovered several cave complexes that had been utilised by the enemy. Conducting SSE, the paratroopers discovered arms caches and sets of documents. SOF demolition experts attached to the QRF destroyed all of the weapons in place so that they could not be used against Coalition forces. According to CJTF-180 spokesman Col Roger King, 'They found proof of use in many of the caves – cooking oil, cigarettes and cigarette butts. They also found several more caches of weapons and pack animals. Operations will continue in the area until all the caves have been thoroughly searched.'

After three days of combat, with Apaches from the 3-229th flying around-the-clock support missions, all the caves had been searched and 80-plus enemy fighters killed or captured by Coalition forces. US infantry units were then withdrawn from the area aboard CH-47s and flown back to Kandahar.

INCREASE IN ATTACKS

Although Taleban and al-Qaeda forces had been dealt some serious blows since 11 September 2001, the organisation began regrouping in the border region of Afghanistan and Pakistan in the early months of 2003. The direct result of this was a series of ever bolder attacks on US and Coalition forces. The ideal combat scenario for Taleban and al-Qaeda fighters was a surprise attack on Coalition troops that lasted just a matter of minutes, during which time they would inflict as many casualties as possible, before disengaging. However, more often than not, US forces would strive to fight through an ambush in order to maintain contact with their elusive foes, calling in for air support from tactical aircraft overhead or QRF Apaches as soon as they were attacked.

On 25 April 2003, while operating near Shkin, elements of the 3rd Battalion, 504th PIR came under fire from concealed positions, killing Pvt Jerod R Dennis and A1C Raymond Losano of the USAF Tactical Air Control Party (TACP), as well as wounding five others. This ambush quickly developed into a sustained ground battle in south-eastern Afghanistan, with the US paratroopers calling for QRF support and Air Force CAS. Once the aircraft were overhead, the remaining members of the TACP deconflicted the airspace above, coordinating Apache strikes on enemy positions with bombing runs from USAF F-16s and A-10s.

Two weeks later, a combined US SOF and ANA patrol was attacked at night with small-arms and RPG fire while returning from a reconnaissance mission in the vicinity of Khowst. A Coalition QRF from FOB 'Chapman' was rapidly on-scene, inserting a ground force, while a 'Tigers' fire team provided escort and overhead security. Establishing a perimeter, friendly forces moved into the compound from where the fire had originated, but the killing of an ANA soldier by further enemy rounds convinced the QRF to hold off their final assault until first light. At dawn, the force duly stormed the compound, with Apaches supporting them with 30 mm cannon rounds. The site was soon in Coalition hands, QRF troops having killed two enemy fighters and wounded a third.

Early June saw Coalition troops returning to the Shah-i-Kot valley for the first time in over a year after intelligence sources had discovered that a new anti-Afghan force was gathering for an attack on the loya jirga (grand council) in Kabul, led by President Hamid Karzai. The response to this new threat was immediate, with the launching of Operation *Dragon Fury* on 2 June. Units from both the 82nd Airborne and 10th Mountain Divisions were combat air assaulted into the valley in a series of blocking moves very similar in their execution to the ambitious, but unsuccessful, Operation *Anaconda* of March 2002.

Dragon Fury was the first brigade-sized offensive launched in Afghanistan in nearly a year, with US troop ranks being swelled by the participation of the Italian Army's mechanised Task Force *Nibbio*. The latter moved into the Shah-i-Kot and manned various blocking positions along the valley. Once all these forces were in place, the 505th PIR air assaulted into the valley and attempted to drive enemy fighters towards the blocking positions. This classical 'hammer-and-anvil' tactic had been employed during *Anaconda* and failed. However, this would not be the case in *Dragon Fury*.

'Flying Tigers' fire teams were heavily involved right from the start of the offensive, staging from both 'Orgun-E' and Bagram in order to support the assault. Apache crews hit targets along the Afghanistan–Pakistan border in coordination with infantry and SOF teams on the ground. On 3 June 'Flying Tigers' AH-64A 89-0258 went down at 1330 hrs while supporting combat operations north-west of 'Orgun-E'. The crew emerged from the wreckage of their helicopter with relatively minor injuries, and were flown to the US Army Combat Support Hospital at Bagram. Their Apache was not so lucky, however, and its shattered hulk was destroyed in place a day later by SOF demolition teams.

As with *Anaconda*, the renewed offensive in the Shah-i-Kot valley was conducted to locate, isolate and destroy al-Qaeda and Taleban militias suspected of still operating in this area. Although this operation was militarily successful, it caused enemy forces to hastily change their tactics. Realising that they could not trade blows with better-armed Coalition troops, the fighters instead attacked a crowd of unarmed civilians on the road from Khowst to Gardez on 5 June, critically wounding several of them. This action prompted a second round of air assaults into the Shah-i-Kot by US forces, resulting in further rocket attacks on friendly bases in the vicinity.

On 20 July AH-64s again inflicted heavy losses on Taleban fighters when they responded to an

AH-64A 90-0260 *DAMAGE INC.* was another of the 'Tigersharks' aircraft handed over to the 3rd Battalion, 229th Attack Helicopter Regiment (*1Sgt Rick Szlachta*)

A soldier from 1-130 AVN cleans the dust off an Apache at Bagram air base in September 2003 (*US Army*)

A lone 1-130th Task Force *Panther* AH-64A conducts a patrol over the Afghan foothills (*US Army*)

attack on a Coalition convoy near the border town of Spin Boldak. Up to 24 enemy soldiers were killed, as a US statement released at the time from Bagram air base revealed:

'The Coalition forces drove through the Taleban's kill zone, requested close air support and engaged the enemy forces, killing approximately five enemy and pursuing the remaining forces into the surrounding hills. AH-64 Apaches provided the air support, making several passes on one particular hill and killing approximately 17–19 more enemy.'

ARMY NATIONAL GUARD INTO ACTION

The 3rd Battalion, 229th Aviation's cessation of operations in-theatre in August 2003 marked the end of a major phase in OEF, for the unit's replacements would be the first Army National Guard (ARNG) attack helicopter battalion committed to the active war on terror. With frontline Army units now firmly focused on fighting the conflict in Iraq, responsibility for continuing the campaign in Afghanistan would fall to ARNG units activated soon after the 11 September 2001 attacks.

The 1st Battalion, 130th Aviation from the North Carolina ARNG arrived at Kandahar in August following an eight-month work-up period at Fort Hood. Well trained and eager to get into the fight, the 'Panthers' seamlessly took over from the 3-229th AVN and proceeded to conduct operations in much the same way as their predecessors had done.

One significant difference, however, was the creation of Task Force *Panther*, which included Active and Reserve component aviation units from the active duty 10th Mountain Division, North Carolina ARNG and Army Reserves. These somewhat dissimilar organisations were soon operating like a well-oiled machine, conducting combat air assaults throughout the eastern regions of Afghanistan. As 1-130th AVN's C Company commander, Capt Benny F Collins, explained at the time, 'Our ultimate goal is to effectively support ground forces, to have great communication between the two, and to hit the right targets quickly.'

One of the biggest changes the 'Panthers' had to get used to was the return to 'running fire' tactics created during Vietnam, which most pilots in the unit had not practiced prior to their pre-deployment work-ups. Capt Collins recalled:

'The heat, combined with the altitude, and the enemy situation, just didn't allow us to hover in Afghanistan. You could train for these types of operations as much as you wanted to back home, but until you flew in-theatre, you hadn't trained in those types of conditions.'

The 'Panthers'' first shots fired in anger came in the early hours of 1 August 2003 when four insurgents were killed in a firefight with a US SOF squad north of Kandahar. American and Coalition troops were in the process of investigating a compound when they took fire from a platoon-sized (ten to 12 men) element of insurgents several hundred metres away. A call was quickly made to the Apache QRF at Kandahar, and a short while later a fire team of 'Panthers' AH-64s was overhead, engaging the insurgents who had dug in on a ridgeline, killing four of them with 30 mm cannon fire.

'Panthers' combat missions continued at a steadily increasing pace as enemy activity increased throughout the summer. An unusual encounter happened on 31 August when a Sports Utility Vehicle (SUV), apparently driven by two insurgents, attempted to take on a 'Panthers' Apache 'one-on-one' on the outskirts of Bagram. The truck, manoeuvring erratically, began speeding aggressively toward Coalition forces engaged in combat operations in Paktika province. Not cleared to fire, the Apache's crew placed their aircraft between the oncoming vehicle and friendly forces, attempting to dissuade the driver from getting any closer to the action. This had no effect, however, and the vehicle continued its dash towards Coalition troops.

With its intentions clearly hostile, the SUV was engaged by the AH-64's co-pilot/gunner, who hit it with the helicopter's 30 mm cannon. The vehicle came to an immediate halt and the Apache crew broke off their attack and made a pass over the SUV in order to perform a quick battle damage assessment. The two men who had been in the vehicle had by then taken refuge in a nearby ditch, and although they were spotted making their escape on foot, the Apache crew was ordered to disengage and return to the ongoing battle. With the AH-64 back on station overhead, Coalition forces disengaged shortly thereafter.

MOUNTAIN VIPER

The end of August also brought renewed large-scale operations, specifically Operation *Mountain Viper*. This involved a combined US and Afghan sweep of Zabul province, and particularly the Dey Chopan area. Like *Anaconda* and *Dragon Fury* before it, *Mountain Viper's* primary objective was to eliminate Taleban and al-Qaeda insurgents in the areas east of Kandahar.

The operation began with an infantry company of the 10th Mountain Division's 'Warrior' Brigade air assaulting into the mountains north of Dey Chopan. Apaches not only provided security for these air assaults, but also collected essential intelligence by flying reconnaissance missions in the area well ahead of the assault force. TADS/PNVS imagery was then utilised to assess both enemy troop strengths and the feasibility of various potential LZs.

Upon initiating the operation, SOF units attached to the ANA pushed towards the 10th Mountain's AO and duly ran headlong into a platoon-sized element of Taleban and al-Qaeda fighters. Engaging them, and calling for Apache support, the combined arms team was able to kill at least eight enemy troops before forcing them to withdraw. The following day, the same battle plan was repeated in a slightly different area, and Coalition troops were again involved in several sharp firefights with a significant number of enemy soldiers.

Mountain Viper came to an end on 3 September, by which time US and Afghan forces had systematically cleared numerous cave complexes and inflicted serious losses on al-Qaeda and Taleban forces in a series of

firefights. During the fighting, the 'Panthers' Apaches worked closely with ground forces to eliminate dug-in positions. USAF A-10s were also routinely on station overhead, and they worked in tandem with Apaches to eliminate the greatest threats with AGM-65 Maverick missiles and 30 mm Avenger cannon.

During the fighting on the final day of *Mountain Viper*, a Hellfire missile fired by a 'Panthers' Apache hit a suspected Taleban and al-Qaeda rally point, killing a number of combatants and effectively decapitating the unit's leadership. After that strike, the enemy fled in disarray, thus ending the operation, and any significant enemy presence in the area. It is estimated that the four days of combat cost enemy forces between 80 and 90 fighters killed and an untold number wounded.

As a 1-211th AVN AH-64A flies overhead, Humvees from Battalion Landing Team 1st Battalion, 6th Marines cross a wide, fast-moving river in south-central Afghanistan on 12 July 2004. This unit had inflicted heavy casualties on the enemy in this area the previous month (*USMC*)

This 1-211th AVN AH-64A was photographed en route to 'Orgun-E' from Kandahar. After three years of operations, Apaches are still flying daily combat missions in Afghanistan (*211th Aviation*)

The 130th continued to fly daily combat missions in support of TFs *Panther* and *Nighthawk* for the remainder of its time in Afghanistan, although the unit would not be in major contact with the enemy again. The battalion remained in-theatre until late spring 2004, when it was replaced by units from the Florida and Utah ANGs as part of OEF IV.

JOINT OPERATIONS

The troop rotations of OEF IV in the spring of 2004 coincided with a complete reorganisation of all Army and Marine air assets in Afghanistan. The end result was the formation of a Joint Task Force (JTF) Wings command structure under the control of the 25th Aviation Brigade's CO, Col Shannon Davis. The task force has direct control over all rotary wing aviation operations within Afghanistan, which at that time consisted of Army active duty and ARNG units, as well as two Marine Forces Reserve helicopter squadrons.

As with the aviation assets that preceded them in Afghanistan, the units that currently form the 2000-man JTF Wings are tasked with flying missions around the clock in support of ground forces at locations across the country.

The creation of JTF Wings came at a time when Multinational Stabilisation Force operations in

Since the attack helicopter mission in Afghanistan had historically been a battalion-level undertaking, the two incoming companies of AH-64s from Utah and Florida were augmented by Marine Forces Reserve AH-1W Super Cobra squadron HMLA-773 from Marietta, Georgia, which operated from FOB 'Salerno' (*HMLA-773*)

Afghanistan were proceeding well, and combat flare-ups had tailed off considerably.

Taking these factors into consideration, Army planners decided in early 2004 that two companies of AH-64s could effectively cover the entire country, freeing up attack assets for other deployments, or later unit rotations. The Florida-based 'Hog Hunters' of B Company, 111th AVN, and the 'Buccaneers' of B Company, 211th AVN, Utah ARNG, were tasked with performing the close combat attack and escort mission from April onwards.

Since the attack helicopter mission in Afghanistan had historically been a battalion-level undertaking, the two incoming companies of AH-64s from Utah and Florida (based at Kandahar and Bagram, respectively) were augmented by Marine Forces Reserve AH-1W Super Cobra squadron HMLA-773 from Marietta, Georgia, which operated from FOB 'Salerno'.

An interesting result of the Army–Marine cooperation in JTF Wings was the return of the 'Heavy Hog' armament configuration on Army helicopters. Since its acceptance into service, the Apache's primary weapon has been the AGM-114 Hellfire anti-tank missile. Yet, with the primary targets in Afghanistan having been personnel and a single SUV to date, the need for carrying expensive Hellfire rounds was called into question. Borrowing from Marine stocks, Army AH-64s began utilising four M261 19-shot rocket pods, loaded with a mix of M151 10-lb and M229 17-lb HE rockets and M255 flechettes for anti-personnel use.

Operations in the spring and early summer of 2004 focused on civil policing and the provision of military support for the introduction of political stabilisation throughout the country. Air assault missions gave way to relief efforts like Operation *Shoe-Fly*, organised by the 1-211th Attack and 1-214th Combat Support Aviation battalions, where donations of shoes from the US were brought to remote villages by helicopter and distributed to Afghan children.

However, combat mission tempo increased sharply in the opening days of June after Taleban and al-Qaeda elements fired small arms and RPGs at Marine AH-1W Super Cobras acting as scouts for a 22nd Marine Expeditionary Unit convoy operating in south-central Afghanistan. A mechanised Battalion Landing Team from the 1st Battalion, 6th Marines moved quickly to engage Taleban units, and called for additional air support while advancing on the enemy positions. Fixed-wing CAS took the form of Marine AV-8B Harrier IIs and Air Force A-10s, while the Army Apaches worked in conjunction with the already present Super Cobra fire team. Thanks to their well-camouflaged positions, the enemy forces managed to exchange fire with the Marines on the ground for almost four hours before finally being forced to withdraw. They left behind eight bodies as proof of the air support's effectiveness.

Operations in Afghanistan have taken on a new dimension, as ARNG AH-64s are now flying support missions for Marine Corps units. Here, a 1-211th AVN crew provide security for elements of Battalion Landing Team 1st Battalion, 6th Marines as they push deep into Afghanistan's Oruzgan province on 27 June 2004 during Operation *Thunder Road* (*USMC*)

Marines from Marine Wing Support Squadron 473 duck for cover from flying stones as an AH-64 from 1-211th AVN lands near FOB 'Orgun-E' on 12 October 2004 (*USMC*)

The following morning, Army Apaches, having taken over from the Marine fire team, scouted ahead of the column and located a platoon-sized element of Taleban fighters attempting to flee the area. After making a positive identification that these were in fact enemy troops, the two AH-64s rolled in and engaged them with 30 mm cannon in an effort to slow their escape and allow the Marine convoy to engage them.

Aircraft from all three services again showed up on-scene and expended ordnance as large as a 2000-lb JDAM bomb, dropped by a B-1B. Seventeen enemy troops were killed in the engagement and the remainder were captured.

On 28 June JTF Wings lost its first Apache near the town of Qalat, some 240 miles south-west of Kabul, in the Zabul province, after the crew declared an in-flight emergency when the APU FIRE indicator lit up in the pilot's cockpit. He was forced to make an emergency landing, and the resulting fire completely destroyed the aircraft after the crew had evacuated their blazing Apache with minor injuries.

Skirmishes with Taleban insurgents continued through July and August. Often, the mere presence of an AH-64 overhead caused enemy forces to either disengage or refrain from initiating contact altogether. In mid-July, after attacking a Coalition patrol, four insurgents turned-tail and ran once they became aware that the Apache QRF was en route. According to JTF Wings commander Col Davis, 'The AH-64 is quite an intimidating platform. When the anti-Coalition militia see it out there in the field, they know that the aircraft is so mobile that we can effectively cross any ridgeline and any river at a moment's notice. Many of them have seen the "business end" of this aircraft, so when the AH-64 is in the area, it really brings a calm to things.'

As of the spring of 2005, JTF Wings AH-64As continue to provide aerial fire support to Coalition ground forces in Afghanistan. Their tour will be ending shortly, and the first US-manned AH-64D units (six AH-64Ds of the Royal Netherlands Air Force's No 301 Sqn deployed to Afghanistan in late March 2004) will soon be deployed to take over OEF responsibilities from them. The exemplary performance of ARNG Apache units has been a testament to the citizen soldiers called up for the War on Terror.

COLOUR PLATES

1
AH-64A 88-0209 of A Company, 3-101 ATKHB, 101st Airborne Division, Bagram, Afghanistan, March 2002

2
AH-64A 90-0288 of A Company, 3-101 ATKHB, 101st Airborne Division, Bagram, Afghanistan, March 2002

3
AH-64A 89-0245 *DELIVERANCE* of B Company, 1-229 ATKHB, XVIII Airborne Corps, Bagram, Afghanistan, November 2002

4
45.AH-64A 88-0202 *DEVIL'S DANCE* of C Company, 1-229 ATKHB, XVIII Airborne Corps, Kandahar, Afghanistan, autumn 2002

5
AH-64A 89-0260 *DAMAGE INC.* of C Company, 3-229 ATKHB, XVIII Airborne Corps, Kandahar, Afghanistan, early 2003

6
AH-64D 99-5102 of B Company, 1-3 ATKHB, 3rd Infantry Division, southern Iraq, 20 March 2003

7
AH-64D 99-5118 of C Company, 1-3 ATKHB, 3rd Infantry Division, An Nasiriyah, Iraq, 31 March 2003

8
AH-64D 98-5061 of 1-101 ATKHB, 101st Airborne Division, Mosul, Iraq, late April 2003

9
AH-64D 97-5032 of A Company, 2-101 ATKHB, 101st Airborne Division, Mosul, Iraq, summer 2003

10
AH-64D 99-5135 of C Company, 1-227 ATKHB, 1st Cavalry Division, OPCONNed to 11th Aviation Regiment (Attack),
Karbala, Iraq, 24 March 2003

11
AH-64D 00-5220 of B Troop, 6-6th Cavalry, 11th Aviation Regiment (Attack), Karbala, Iraq, 24 March 2003

12
AH-64D 00-5211 of A Troop, 6-6th Cavalry, 11th Aviation Regiment (Attack), Karbala, Iraq, 24 March 2003

13
AH-64A 86-8955 of A Troop, 2-6th Cavalry, 11th Aviation Regiment (Attack), Objective *Talon*, Iraq, April 2003

14
AH-64D 01-5241 of C Company, 1-4th ATKHB, 4th Infantry Division, Tikrit, Iraq, autumn 2003

15
AH-64A 87-0425 of B Company, 1-501st ATKHB, 1st Armored Division, Balad, Iraq, January 2004

16
AH-64A 88-0197 of C Company, 1-501st ATKHB, 1st Armored Division, Baghdad, Iraq, December 2003

17
AH-64A 87-0428 of A Company, 1-1st ATKHB, 1st Infantry Division, Irbil, Iraq, October 2004

18
AH-64A 87-0474 of B Company, 1-1st ATKHB, 1st Infantry Division, FOB 'Speicher', Iraq, December 2004

19
AH-64D 02-5296 of A Company, 1-227th ATKHB, 1st Cavalry Division, Balad, Iraq, November, 2004

20
AH-64A 87-0453 of 1-130th ATKHB, North Carolina Army National Guard, Kandahar, Afghanistan, January 2004

21
AH-64A 94-0332 of 1-151st ATKHB, South Carolina Army National Guard, Mosul, Iraq, December 2004

OPERATION *IRAQI FREEDOM*

The failure to reach a diplomatic solution to the Iraqi resistance to United Nations' arms inspections in the winter of 2002–2003 set events in motion that culminated in the mid-March 2003 ultimatum for President Saddam Hussein to relinquish power or face an invasion by US and British forces. On 20 March, acting on a credible intelligence tip, two USAF F-117A Nighthawks hit a pinpoint target with four 2000-lb JDAM guided bombs in the hope of killing Saddam, and therefore 'decapitating' the Iraqi command and control network.

As the stealth fighter crews were receiving their targeting information for their strike on Baghdad, pilots of the 3rd Infantry Division's 1st Battalion, 3rd Aviation Regiment (nicknamed the 'Vipers') were about to conduct their final rehearsals before the invasion, which was supposed to occur the following day. According to 'Vipers'' B Company commander Capt Rogelio Garcia, 'When we walked in to the rehearsal, the brigade commander, Col Curtis Potts, asked if we could execute in 30 minutes!'

Due to the immediacy of the 'decapitation strike' information, all invasion plans had been advanced 24 hours, thus initiating a chain reaction of events that would have two companies from the 'Vipers'' airborne from Camp Udairi, in Kuwait, within an hour of receiving their warning order. The mission was essential for the success of the entire invasion, as Iraqi forces had established several observation and command posts along the border as an early-warning system in the face of the impending invasion. B and C Companies of 1-3 AVN were each tasked with observing the impact of artillery fires on these targets, after which they were to eliminate any posts that appeared to remain operable.

The 'Warlords' of B Company were assigned the five northernmost targets, consisting of two command and three observation posts. Capt Garcia (call-sign 'Warlord 06') split his company into two fire teams. Team 1, with four Apaches, was commanded by 1Lt Mike Labroad ('Warlord 26'). It was tasked with the observation and destruction of four targets, as well as serving as a communications relay between Team 2 and brigade operations. Team 2 consisted of Capt Garcia's aircraft, flown by CW4 George Lutz, and his wingmen, CW4 Gary Fewins and co-pilot/gunner CW2 Mike Roman ('Warlord 09'). They would eliminate the two most distant, and difficult, targets. 'Warlord 23', flown by CW2s Steve Sheahan and Rob Phillips, had a TADS/PNVS malfunction on start-up, and since it was a night mission, they were unable to launch, leaving Team 1 with three AH-64Ds.

Capt Garcia recounted how the operation played out:

'Everyone in the battalion understood the importance of this mission. These observation and command posts were there to report any sign of

A 2nd Battalion, 101st Aviation AH-64D is offloaded from a US Navy transport ship in Kuwait in February 2003 (*US Army*)

'Warlord 06' and 'Outcast 06', alias Capts Rogelio 'R J' Garcia and Scott Myers, relax with cigars between missions (*Capt 'R J' Garcia*)

our invasion. The northern command post (my team's target) was isolated, barely in communications range for our radios and ten kilometres inside Iraq. It was originally supposed to be destroyed by USAF close-air support aircraft, but due to changes in the Air Tasking Order (ATO), we were assigned to take it out instead. The target was also within 500 metres of a UN compound. Its destruction was critical to the success of the mission – it could not go undestroyed. I knew that every one of my crews could have done it, but if something went wrong, I wanted to be responsible for the failure.

'Once at the border, we were to hold and pass confirmation that we had eyes on the target, verifying that it was in fact there, and clear of any civilians. Additionally, my team had to confirm the existence of the UN building. Once confirmation was sent, we waited for the artillery to impact. Coincidentally, as we were waiting for the latter, cruise missiles were flying above us on their way to targets in Baghdad, and USAF jets were crossing the border heading north. Our brigade and battalion S-3 (Operations) "shops" did an amazing job deconflicting airspace by time, altitude and location so that all assets could execute their missions effectively.

'At 1800 Z (2100 hrs local time), the artillery rounds impacted their targets. Once we were told that all rounds had been fired, we were cleared to cross into Iraq and observe the targets and respond as needed. We all crossed the border and found that the artillery had been right on target. However, because there could be no question as to whether the targets had been destroyed or not, every building had to be serviced again to ensure their total destruction. Once all the targets were confirmed destroyed, both companies returned safely to Camp Udairi to refuel and rearm.'

During the engagement, the first AGM-114L Radar Frequency (RF) Hellfire III missile was fired in combat by AH-64D 'Warlord 19', flown by CW3 Chad Breidenstein and CW2 Matt Roe. Interestingly, the Longbow radar was not used in this engagement, the crew instead performing a 'laser transfer' that saw CW2 Roe designating the target with the Apache's laser designator and then passing the data to the missile's internal radar, which in turn acquired the target. Once the missile had locked on, CW2 Roe fired and destroyed the targeted building.

The 'Outcasts' of C Company enjoyed similar success on the first night of the conflict. Capt Scott Myers' company launched five aircraft, with the sixth remaining behind due to serviceability problems. Myers led a heavy team with wingmen Rob Purdy and Sean McNeal to observe the artillery impacts in their sector, before heading in to engage the observations posts in much the same way as B Company had done to the north.

This 1-3 AVN AH-64D carries a typical OIF weapons load out, consisting of a 19-shot M261 rocket pod (this one is not fully loaded) and four Hellfire III missiles, three of which were semi-active laser K models and one was an AGM-114L radar frequency round – the latter is seen here adorned with graffiti. An identical weapons load would be carried beneath the Apache's starboard stub wing (*CW3 Michael S Madura*)

A 'Vipers' AH-64D hovers over a knocked-out T-54 tank while searching for new targets in southern Iraq in the early days of OIF. The 'Vipers' were the first to score a tank kill with the radar-frequency-guided AGM-114L Hellfire III when a B Company 'Warlords' Apache knocked out a T-54 similar to this one on 21 March 2003 (*US Army*)

According to CW3 Purdy, 'The artillery fire was ineffective, so we destroyed the targets ourselves. There was no stiff resistance – just some small-arms fire and maybe an RPG or two, but nothing serious'.

As the invading force moved into Iraq, 'Vipers' Apaches ranged ahead of the advancing division, engaging Iraqi armour at will, spotting for artillery fires and providing forward reconnaissance for the division. CW3 Purdy recalled:

'The ground brigades moved so fast. We were on their flanks at times and out front at times. We rotated companies, and sometimes teams, to support whatever ground commander was in contact.'

The battalion was heavily engaged in air support missions for American infantry during the close-quarters street fighting for control of the city of An Nasiriyah. CW3 Purdy explained how operations worked in this environment for Apache crews:

'Obviously, you had to have an absolutely positive visual ID on the frontline trace of friendlies. Once you had that, it was a free for all. We would take target handovers from guys on the ground using IR pointers and eight-digit grid coordinates, engaging targets anywhere from four kilometres out to just 200-300 metres from friendly positions. Most of the bad guys quickly took their uniforms off. They would wave white flags until you got to within 300 metres of them and then they would open fire. This inevitably meant that we were operating close in to friendly forces.'

During the initial drive northward, Bravo Company scored the first tank kill for the Longbow Apache and the new radar missile on 21 March when a 'Warlords' aircraft engaged and destroyed a T-54 tank with a radar-frequency-guided Hellfire III. More T-54s and T-55s were encountered, along with MT-LB amoured personnel carriers (APCs), but the majority of mobile targets were 'technicals' – Toyota pick-up trucks with 0.50-calibre machine guns or HOT anti-tank missiles bolted to their beds. While these may have been somewhat troublesome for troops on the ground, they were simply cannon fodder for the advancing Apaches.

One of the 'Viper' Battalion's most memorable missions in OIF occurred on 22 March, as the unit's S-3 operations officer, Maj David Rude, explained:

'At approximately 1200 hrs local, a "Viper" team of two Apaches had successfully completed a medevac security escort mission west of the city of An Nasiriyah, home to the Iraqi Army's 11th Infantry Division, as well as a stronghold for Fedayeen loyalists. As the AH-64Ds were returning to base at Objective "Charlie" (Jalibah air base), they received an in-flight mission to conduct a search and attack in order to locate and destroy two suspected Iraqi D-30 artillery howitzers south of Tallil air base.

'Upon arriving at the initial search site, the "Viper" team leader received a distress call over the command radio net from an infantry officer on the ground, call-sign "Battle Three". The ground element, consisting of two Hummers, two M2A2 Bradley Fighting Vehicles and one M1A2 Main Battle Tank, was pinned down by heavy enemy fire, and they had already taken several casualties.

'Without regard for their own safety, the two "Viper" crews – CWOs Tom Nowlin, Jessie Oliver, Kory Hawkinson and Brent Huntsman from A Company "Assassins" – gallantly flew to within 500 metres of the enemy location in order to provide immediate fire support to shield the friendly vehicles from further Iraqi fire. Despite taking direct fire from enemy SAMs, anti-aircraft artillery and small arms, the AH-64s continued their destructive onslaught with decisive 30 mm cannon, 2.75-in rockets and Hellfire missile engagements against an unforgiving force.

'Throughout the action, a soldier on the ground provided navigational reference calls to the Apache team on the radio, as well as directing 25 mm fire from his Bradley Fighting Vehicle to orient the Apaches to the most critical enemy threat – three Anti-Tank Guided Missile (ATGM) systems, which were located near a bridge on the main convoy route. The "Viper" team's effective fire and manoeuvre enabled the destruction of the ATGM sites, one machine gun, four gunboats, one cargo vehicle in defilade, one cargo truck full of ammunition and 25 enemy personnel. The "Vipers" remained on station providing security and support by fire to the ground elements until all enemy threats were eliminated.

'The timely Apache fire support against determined Fedayeen forces, which had employed unconventional tactics, prevented friendly ground troops from taking addi-

On 22 March 2003, these two 'Vipers' crews (from left to right, CWOs Tom Nowlin, Jessie Oliver, Kory Hawkinson and Brent Huntsman) from A Company 'Assassins' gallantly flew to within 500 metres of an enemy position near Tallil air base in order to provide immediate fire support to shield friendly vehicles from further Iraqi fire. Despite taking direct fire from SAMs, AAA and small-arms, the AH-64 crews pressed home their destructive onslaught with decisive 30 mm cannon, 2.75-in rockets and Hellfire missile engagements against an unforgiving force (*CW3 Michael S Madura*)

1-3 AVN's 'Viper 10' returns from a kill (smoking in the background) west of Baghdad while securing the 3rd ID's western flank in early April 2003 (*CW3 Michael S Madura*)

CW2s Tom Higgins and Jeremy Herrera from 'Assassin' Troop, 6-6th Cavalry pose for the camera at Camp Udairi, Kuwait, prior to heading north into Iraq (*Assassincountry.org*)

AH-64D 00-5232 crashed soon after taking off from the FARP near Najaf on the night of 23 March 2003. The helicopter's crew, CW2s Higgins and Herrera, had suffered total brown-out in the swirling dust soon after lifting off in the heavy AH-64. They were heading for Karbala to attack the Republican Guard's Medina Division in the desert south of the city. Neither crewman was injured, and the Apache was subsequently repaired and returned to service (*Assassincountry.org*)

tional fire and casualties. All the participating Apache crewmen received Air Medals with Valor for their extraordinary efforts during this mission.'

DEEP ATTACK – KARBALA

As V Corps' 3rd Infantry Division drove northwards into Iraq from Kuwait, its attached aviation unit – 11th Aviation Helicopter Regiment (AHR) – was planning its attack on the Republican Guard Medina Division. The latter was occupying ground between the town of Hillah and the city of Karbala, defending key terrain that the Iraqi high command knew had to be taken by US forces in order for them to continue their advance on Baghdad. It was determined that a regimental-strength deep attack mission conducted by three battalions of AH-64s from the 11th Aviation Regiment would be ideal for wearing down, if not outright destroying, the division.

Staging from Camp Udairi, the regiment's two cavalry squadrons – 2-6 and 6-6 Cavalry, and the attached 1-227th ATKHB on loan from the 1st Cavalry Division – moved to a FARP established at an Iraqi airstrip on the outskirts of the city of Najaf.

The mission ran into difficulty right from the start. The regiment's supply convoy, also headed north from Camp Udairi, was late in arriving at the FARP due to invasion traffic along the major avenues of approach. When the mission go-ahead was given, only the 227th's supply convoy had arrived at the FARP, and it did not have enough fuel and weaponry to get the entire regiment mission-ready. The 18 AH-64Ds of the 1-227th ATKHB were fuelled and armed first, followed by 13 Apaches from 6-6 Cavalry. This left the mission force 23 helicopters short of full-strength. 2-6 Cavalry, which was to have acted as the reserve battalion, would not participate in the action. It would remain at the FARP instead, securing the base from possible Iraqi counter-attacks. The squadron would see action a few days later.

Understrength, the regiment's two battalions struggled to get airborne in the swirling dust, the latter causing a number of near-misses in both battalions. At 0122 hrs local time, B Troop, 6-6 Cavalry launched six aircraft for the mission, followed by A Troop. 'Assassin' Troop's Apache 00-5232 crashed on take-off after entering complete brown-out conditions, its crew, CW2s Tom Higgins and Jeremy Herrera, escaping unharmed. The aircraft was later salvaged, but it was one fewer Apache that would be able to put fire downrange against the Medina Division.

The two battalions' 30 Apaches formed up in their respective fire teams and headed north towards Karbala. When they visually acquired the city, it was clear something was afoot as it was in near darkness, even though it was the middle of the night. Intermittent ground fire began to increase steadily as they approached Karbala, and suddenly all the remaining lights were switched off.

CW2 Bill Neal and CW4 Bob Duffney led Bravo Troop's assault in AH-64D 00-5220, and flying on their wing was 1Lt Jason King ('Pale Rider 16') and CW2 Mike Tomblin. King, sitting in the front seat of his Apache, had a clear view of the city. 'As we were turning towards the target, all the lights in the city went out for about two seconds. Then they came back on, and the AAA just erupted.'

Calls of 'Taking fire!' began sounding over the radio net as the crews manoeuvred their machines to avoid the incoming rounds. After the initial eruption of AAA, ground fire remained accurate for the entire 45-minute period that the 11th's Apaches were overhead, prompting some to claim that the defenders had some form of night vision capability. Others have suggested that since the night was overcast, the aircraft were silhouetted against the clouds, but either way, the strike force's aircraft were visible to the enemy, and taking hits because of it.

During the fray, King and Tomblin's Apache was hit by a burst of AK-47 fire which penetrated the cockpit and struck the former in the throat as he was calling out fires. Although wounded, King was able to maintain consciousness and apply a pressure dressing. He was initially unable to speak, so CW2 Tomblin could not determine his status. As they egressed the battlefield, escorted by Neal and Duffney (the last two Apaches from the 6-6th to leave the area), Tomblin set the Apache down in a field outside of Najaf to assess King's injuries. King had been extremely lucky, for the bullet had missed his carotid artery by only a matter of millimetres. Following their return to base, King was sent to Germany for surgery, but he returned to B Troop, and flight status, just a few weeks later.

The 1-227th, meanwhile, was having an even more difficult time, braving murderous AAA for little result. Flying AH-64D 97-5025, CW2s Joe Goode and Cindy Rosel were inbound to the target as part of a B Company fire team when their leader engaged the first vehicles that he had spotted. Goode then remembers that, 'The city erupted in gunfire all around us. Before we knew it we were scattered, performing evasive manoeuvres.' Losing sight of one another, the teams quickly lost their mutual support. It was now every crew for themselves. Goode continued:

'We took fire again. And as crazy as it sounds, the fire from that 57 mm S60 AAA was spectacular. It all lasted only momentarily, as we broke down to cover again, all the while jinking left and right to avoid

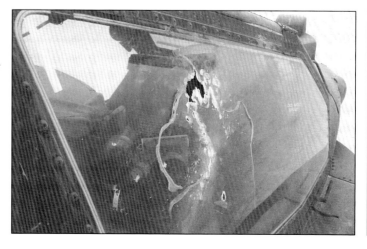

The AH-64D of CW2 Tomblin and 1Lt King was badly shot up by AAA on the night of 23 March during the ill-fated attack on the Medina Division near the Karbala gap. King, sat in the Apache's front cockpit, was struck in the throat by the AK-47 round which caused this damage to his helicopter (*CW2 Bill Neal*)

49

This still taken from Iraqi television shows AH-64D 99-5135 on the ground outside Karbala after being downed by intense enemy fire from the Republican Guard's Medina Division. Pilots CW2s Ronald Young and David Williams were captured shortly after safely landing their damaged Apache behind enemy lines (*Iraqi television*)

fire. We brought the helicopter out of the pattern we were circling in and turned south-west. With Cindy pointing out fire, I pulled in all the power I could muster and drove the cyclic forward. "Colombo 025" was blasting the leaves off palm trees and the sand off rooftops as we got out of there.'

Goode and Rosel were the luckiest crew on the Karbala mission. Despite being fired at hundreds of times, their Apache was the only aircraft of the 30 that participated that did not get hit. The battalion destroyed several Medina Division vehicles, but the AAA soon became too intense and the Apaches had to break off.

The other companies of the 227th fared much worse. The 'Vampires' of C Company found themselves in the most intense sector of the battlefield, and as the Apaches' evasive manoeuvres increased, cohesion between the fire teams completely evaporated. During the fight, Longbow 99-5135, flown by CW2s Ronald Young and David Williams, took a hit to the Flight Management Computer and was forced to land in a field south of the city. Most of their ordnance was still aboard when the AH-64D went down – mute testament to the ferocity of the AAA coming up at the attacking force. Almost immediately other 'Vampires' pilots attempted to land and rescue the two downed fliers, but after two attempts by 227th aviators, heavy AAA forced them to withdraw.

Williams and Young evaded along a nearby canal after coming down, but they were soon spotted by Iraqi civilians after swimming roughly a quarter of a mile downstream. Both men were captured and eventually handed over to Iraqi forces the following morning. They were shown on Iraqi television a short time later, apparently unharmed. The crew would be handed over to US forces in early May following seven weeks in captivity.

Aside from broadcasting pictures of Williams and Young, Iraqi television also claimed that the AH-64 had been brought down by a single round from an old-fashioned bolt-action rifle fired by local peasant farmer Ali Obeid Mengash. However, Central Command's commander-in-chief, Gen Tommy Franks, denied this, stating 'Those events did not occur as a result of farmers.' The destruction of the AH-64D became a major operation for the Coalition, the helicopter being moved by the Iraqis before it could be attacked by an airstrike. It was finally located on 26 March and bombed.

SAFE RETREAT

The remaining 11th Aviation Regiment Apaches made it back to their Tactical Assembly Area (TAA) without further incident. In all, 28 of the surviving 29 aircraft were hit more than once, rendering both battalions combat ineffective for the four days that followed while aircraft were repaired, rotor blades changed and holes patched. The attack claimed a

dozen Iraqi tanks, several soft-skinned vehicles, six S-60 anti-aircraft guns and an untold number of smaller anti-aircraft weaponry destroyed, as well as a significant number of Iraqi troops killed. When the 6-6th Cav and 1-227 ATKHB were deemed combat ready once again, they were tasked with area reconnaissance and convoy escort in the 82nd Airborne's TAOR around Najaf and Hillah.

During OIF, 1-227th ATKHB flew more than 450 combat hours, destroyed 100 + pieces of equipment and killed an estimated 300 personnel, while expending over 100 Hellfires, 800 rockets and 14,000 30 mm rounds, as well as consuming 100,000-plus gallons of JP8 fuel.

101st AIR ASSAULT – HURRY UP AND WAIT

Although delayed in launching its attack, the 101st Airborne Division (Air Assault) began its own 'rendezvous with destiny' by conducting the longest air assault operation ever undertaken. Beginning on 24 March, the division airlifted two brigades to FOB 'Shell', south-east of Karbala, where the 101st would stage from. However, the 3rd Brigade, packed into vehicles just as elements of the 3rd Infantry Division had been, was forced to endure the long drive up from Kuwait.

After the debacle of the 11th AHR's raid on the Medina Division, 101st planners quickly teleconferenced with a number of pilots

CH-47D Chinook and AH-64 Apache pilots from the 101st Airborne Division converse on the flightline at an undisclosed air base in Kuwait shortly before flying to FOB 'Shell', south of Karbala, on 24 March 2003 (*US Army*)

The last week of March halted all Army flight operations due to intense sand storms that limited visibility to less than 50 ft at times. Here, soldiers from 'Assassin' Troop, 6-6th Cavalry congregate together waiting for the weather to clear (*Assassincountry.org*)

Spc Christian Fernandez of B Company, 3rd Battalion, 101st Aviation Regiment cleans the windows of an AH-64 Apache soon after its arrival at FOB 'Shell' on 25 March 2003 (*US Army*)

that had taken part so as not to make the same mistakes when the division's three Apache battalions were committed to combat. Tactics and plans for the three battalions' missions were changed or scrapped, as according to V Corps commander, Lt Gen William Wallace, 'Deep operations with the Apache, unless there's a very, very, very clear need to do it, are probably not a good idea.'

This 'advice', issued to such a large combat unit that focuses on airborne manoeuvrability, and requires the unfettered mobility of its aerial firepower, meant that its operations in the field would be dangerously restrictive.

To further complicate matters, and certainly to the frustration of 101st aircrews, the weather quickly made flying impossible. By 26 March, all helicopter traffic was grounded until the *shamal* sandstorm ended. In order to keep the division's Apaches operable, water had to be pumped through the engines on a near-constant basis so as to prevent the swirling dust from damaging them. Conditions were miserable for air- and groundcrews alike.

While the sandstorm reduced operations to a crawl, planning for the 101st's Apache attack on the Medina Division's 14th Brigade continued its evolution. New avenues of approach were identified, and tighter coordination between pre-strike artillery preparations and the assault element itself emphasised by mission planners. It had been discovered that the 11th AHR's external fire support had been so uncoordinated that it had served only as a warning to the defenders that the AH-64s were inbound.

The 'Wings of Destiny' received the go-ahead for its attack on the 14th Mechanised Brigade on 28 March. The operation, code named *Destiny Reach*, involved the 1st and 2nd Battalions of the 101st Aviation Regiment (both AH-64D-equipped battalions, while the 3rd Battalion, flying AH-64As, would be held in reserve), which would attack from different directions – a move designed to confuse the defenders and maximise the Apache's strengths. The 2nd Battalion would go in first, attacking from the south in a classic 'movement to contact'. Once the battalion's Apaches were engaged, they were ordered to pull back and let USAF and Navy fixed-wing assets hit those targets. In the confusion, the 1st Battalion was to circle north-west of the city and then attack southwards, hitting the brigade in the rear.

With the perceived failure of the 11th AHR five days earlier, there was a great deal of significance attached to the 101st's mission. High-profile defence journalists and fixed-wing proponents alike had severely criticised the effectiveness and survivability of the attack helicopter on the modern battlefield in the wake of the Karbala operation. Such comments had left the 101st's attack pilots in no doubt as to the fact that the very future of the Apache depended on a successful outcome to *Destiny Reach*.

101st UNLEASHED!

The war's second deep attack mission began with a go-ahead from Lt Gen William Wallace. When the code word 'Carrie' was transmitted on the afternoon of 28 March, the final maintenance, loading of ordnance and fuelling of the three battalions was already well underway.

The mission commenced at 2030 hrs local time, when helicopters of both battalions began taking off in the dust created by the rotor wash of nearly 40 Apaches. All of the AH-64s were heavily laden, fully loaded with fuel and maximum ammunition. Within four minutes of the first launch, one of the A Company crews became disoriented and crashed, wrecking their helicopter. The battle had not yet started and the 'Eagle Warriors' had already lost an aircraft.

The remainder of the attack force lifted off without incident and headed north into the darkness. When four minutes out from the target, the new Army Tactical Missile System (ATACMS) launched a barrage to get the defenders' heads down while the Apaches swept in to attack. Unlike the Karbala mission, the defenders did not have time to recover after the barrage before the 2nd Battalion's Apaches were overhead. As planned, when the defenders opened fire on the 'Eagle Warriors' Apaches, the battalion pulled back to a safe distance while fixed-wing CAS aircraft rolled in to fire on the rapidly appearing targets. In the meantime, the 2nd Battalion's Apaches were able to hover, roughly four miles outside of the city, and fire Hellfire missiles at targets of opportunity as they became visible in the TADS/PNVS displays and on NVGs.

Meanwhile, the 1st Battalion had swept in from the north, catching defenders unaware and adding to the confusion on the ground. The entire raid lasted no more than an hour, with both battalions withdrawing just before 2200 hrs local time. The total claimed for the mission amounted to 12 tanks and APCs destroyed, 11 AAA guns of various calibre, three artillery pieces and 20 soft-skinned vehicles. While the operation had been a success materially, it also proved that deep attack missions were still viable for the AH-64, provided they were performed in conjunction with other combined-arms assets. Artillery and close air support that was properly coordinated and teamed with an effective tactical plan proved that the Apache was the deadly deep attack hunter that Boeing professed it to be.

Yet this success had come at a price, for the second loss of the night came at 2128 hrs when AH-64D 97-5032 returned from the mission to FOB 'Shell' for refuelling and rearming. With the Apache's crew disoriented in the wall of sand their rotor wash had kicked up, the aircraft hit the ground too hard and rolled over.

On the night of 28 March 2003, the 101st Airborne launched close to 40 Apaches on an ultimately successful deep attack mission east of Karbala. Two AH-64s crashed, however, both due to their crews suffering from brown-out. Here, AH-64D 97-5032 is illuminated by floodlights soon after it rolled over at FOB 'Shell' following its return from the mission. The aircraft was duly salvaged and repaired (*US Army*)

'VIPERS" OPS

As the 3rd Infantry Division pushed northwards, the 'Vipers' continued to provide both screening and Close Combat Attack (CCA) support to the infantry battalions around An Nasiriyah and An Najaf.

On the morning of 31 March, CW3 Rob Purdy and CW2 Nick DiMona (who was subsequently killed, along with fellow OIF veteran WO1 William Loffer, on 22 June 2004 in an AH-64D crash near Fort Stewart, Georgia) had just returned from a CCA mission in support of

3rd ID infantry units fighting in Najaf. No sooner had the crew shut down AH-64D 99-5118 when their relief, CW3 Cathy Jarrell and CW2 Mike Carman, lifted off on a medevac escort to rescue several critically wounded Marines. However, the Apache's rotor downdraft created a severe brown-out condition, and the main blades of Jarrell and Carman's AH-64D (99-5104) hit the ground and the Apache came down hard. DiMona and Purdy ran over to the shattered helicopter and pulled Jarrell and Carman from the wreckage, as Rob Purdy recalled:

While serving as a QRF for the 3rd ID on 31 March 2003, the crew (CW2 Mike Carman and CW3 Cathy Jarrell) of AH-64D 99-5104 was scrambled on a medevac escort. Moments after lifting off, the aircraft got into brown-out conditions and the main rotor struck the ground, rolling the helicopter onto its back (*US Army*)

'Nick and I had just come off of our QRF shift when our unit got the call to escort the Blackhawk. The crew after us had the mission, but the pilot got into brown-out and rolled the bird over, destroying it. Nick and I quickly pulled them out.'

Luckily, neither Jarrell of Carman was seriously injured, and both would be flying again in the days ahead. The medevac mission, however, was growing more urgent by the minute. Purdy and DiMona ran back to their half-armed and fuelled Apache, began preflight checklists and lifted off as soon as they could.

En route, the Blackhawk's APR-39 radar warning receiver failed, followed quickly by its GPS navigation system, making the mission even more tense. Purdy and DiMona led the medevac helicopter into its pick-up point, and then flew overhead to ensure area security while three American soldiers and two Iraqi civilians were loaded aboard. Once airborne again, the medevac fell into formation with 99-5118 and safely delivered its patients to the Combat Area Surgical Hospital, where they would be treated.

FINAL PUSH NORTHWARDS

As darkness fell on 31 March, the 3rd Infantry Division was gearing up for the final push toward Baghdad. 1-3rd ATKHB was to lead the charge, so the battalion FARP was established well ahead of the division. The battalion's three companies were to rotate in sequence, with each company acting as the 'tip of the spear' for a set period of time. Capt Rains' 'Assassin' Company led off, followed by Garcia's 'Warlords' and Myers' 'Outcasts'. According to Capt Garcia:

'We established a continuous attack. Our mission was CCA, but the most important thing we did for the division was to use our TADS/PNVS range to provide real-time reconnaissance forward of their movement. Alpha Company led off, conducting reconnaissance by fire along the way and undertaking CCA in support of the division's Third Brigade. We relieved them, continuing the mission at a slow to medium pace. There were several key intelligence reports that dictated this. We were told that this was to be Saddam's last stand, and that he had a final protective "red line" that ensured the use of Weapons of Mass Destruction if we crossed it. Because of the enemy situation, all Apache crews were very deliberate in making sure that every enemy defensive position and formation was completely destroyed.

'From an attack helicopter perspective, there was not a major mass target for us to destroy. Everything was "dismounted", making it tough for us to ID. Due to the targets' proximity to our ground troops, we made sure that we had a confirmed identification that we were indeed about to attack an enemy position before going ahead and servicing it.

'Our most important task became to reconnoitre in front of the division as it moved along. Ironically enough, we were able to use the Apache's APG-78 radar for this, as there was so little enemy armour to be detected when we scanned the battlefield, the only thing we picked up was our friendly columns attacking. We achieved incredible situational awareness by scanning and seeing our forces on the radar screen. The radar worked outstandingly well, picking up friendlies in exact formation.

'Right before we were relieved on station, we did receive some small arms, but we were not able to return fire. Our fire team performed a battle handover with C Company, and that was the end of the mission for us. During the after action review, the Division Commander, Gen Blount, and his Assistant Division Commander, thought that the most important task we performed was reconnaissance ahead of the division. Blount's assets were never outgunned, so he didn't need our help with destroying targets, but we were able to provide him with real-time intelligence that his division could act upon immediately.'

Two well-weathered 1-3 AVN AH-64Ds conduct a patrol south of Baghdad in early April 2003 (*CW3 Michael S Madura*)

2-6th CAV INTO COMBAT AT LAST

With the lessons learned from the 23 March raid firmly planted in their minds, the pilots of the 2-6th Cavalry finally entered combat several days later once the fuel and ammunition convoys had arrived at the 11th AHR's FOB. The two battalions that had gone on the ill-fated Karbala mission had been able to repair all but one of their aircraft by the 28th.

'Blackjack' Troop of 2-6th Cavalry pose in front of AH-64A 86-8955 'somewhere in Iraq' (*CPT Joel Magsig*)

As previously mentioned, of the 29 Apaches that made it back to base, only one had escaped damage. Most had been hit a minimum of 15 times with various-calibre projectiles, and more than half of the units' helicopters had bullet holes in their main rotor blades. A few aircraft had even been hit by RPGs,

55

causing damage that certainly would have brought down a less survivable helicopter.

As the remainder of the regiment was returning to flight status, the 2-6th Cav was OPCONNed (operationally controlled) to the 3rd Infantry Division in order to operate as its second attack helicopter battalion. The 2-6th had been scheduled to participate in the Karbala raid, and was finally able to engage Iraqi forces when tasked with reconnaissance and screening operations for the 3rd Infantry Division.

As the division approached Baghdad, infantry and armoured units seized key bridgeheads across the Euphrates. Apaches from both battalions provided overwatch for these forces, guarding against an Iraqi counter-attack during the vulnerable crossing phases. The 2-6th, along with the other two 11th Aviation Regiment battalions, engaged and destroyed between 40 and 50 tanks, APCs and artillery pieces during this phase of the operation, clearing the way for the 3rd Infantry Division and the 101st and 82nd Airborne to press northwards behind them.

In a typical encounter during this phase of the war, on 2 April a 'Blackjack' Troop fire team from the 2-6th was engaged by a platoon-sized element of non-uniformed Saddam Fedayeen on the outskirts of Iskandariyah during a zone reconnaissance mission. Capt Joel Magsig (call-sign 'Blackjack 06') and his back-seater CW2 Terrance Newsome called in a spot report to the 3rd ID HQ and then rolled in, hitting two 'technicals' and killing several Fedayeen. Magsig told the author:

'Two Hellfires and about four rockets later, they stopped shooting at us. We sent a spot report back to the 3rd ID guys about what and where we'd made contact, and I'd like to hope that lives were saved.'

Five days later, Capt Magsig and CW4 Greg Inman were flying a medevac escort back from the frontline when their Apache was struck by several large calibre rounds from a 'technical' hiding amongst a grove of trees. They rolled in to engage the vehicle, but the 0.50-calibre rounds had damaged their fire control system, knocking their weapons offline. The crew disengaged, calling in a spot report to warn other aviation units in the area of the gun's presence.

Needing to assess the damage, the two looked for the closest field to land on. Luckily, Baghdad International Airport (BIAP) had just been taken by the 3rd Infantry Division, although firefights were still raging on the base's periphery. Selecting a taxiway, Inman set the Apache down and both crewmen got out to check the damage. Although one tyre was flat, the tail rotor gearbox had been holed, the radio antenna cut and the fire control system knocked out, the helicopter was still flyable. Unbeknownst to them, their Apache (86-8955) was the first American aircraft to land at BIAP following its capture.

Capt Joel Magsig of 2-6th AVN enjoys a camel ride outside of Baghdad a few days after his historic landing at BIAP on 2 April 2003 (*Capt Joel Magsig*)

The co-pilot/gunner of a sharkmouthed 1-3 AVN AH-64D conducts his preflight checks at an FOB west of Baghdad on 15 April 2003 (*CW3 Michael S Madura*)

The 11th AHR returned to Karbala on 16 April to conduct reconnaissance of the area to ensure that all Republican Guard units had been cleared out. By then the 101st and 82nd Airborne Divisions were pushing northwards through the Karbala gap, where they would run into any remaining Medina Division units. During the operation, the 6-6th Cavalry located 13 ballistic missiles on launchers, aimed southwards. These would be marked for follow-up units to take into custody, while the remainder of the abundant equipment left behind was destroyed by the regiment's Apaches. Surprisingly, many Iraqis on the ground were not shooting, but waving happily as the 11th's Longbows flew over.

Around this same time, B Company, 1-3rd ATKHB, was tasked with flying a zone reconnaissance of the area around Fallujah, west of Baghdad, for the 3rd Infantry Division's 3rd Brigade. Told to stay out of the city of Fallujah itself, the Apache crews were tasked with simply destroying every piece of military equipment they could find. Most of it was unmanned, but it could, potentially, have been very lethal (as demonstrated by the secondary explosions when ammunition racks and fuel exploded from the numerous Hellfire hits) had it gotten into the wrong hands.

After five hours of 'tank plinking', the 'Warlords' were told to cease fire, and that the remaining soft-skinned vehicles they had identified would be salvaged to allow the future Coalition-backed Iraqi Army, National Guard and police force to make use of them post-war.

CAMPAIGN CHANGE

As April wound down, so did major force-on-force combat. Saddam's soldiers seemed to give up and head back to their homes and families, rather than put up a standing fight. By this time, Saddam Fedayeen and foreign fighters comprised the bulk of the forces arrayed against US troops, reducing the armoured threat, but increasing the unpredictability of the conflict. This change in the nature of the campaign directly impacted Apache operations, and caused a further shift towards Vietnam-style tactics, utilising attack helicopters in screening operations ahead of

Downtown Baghdad is seen from the front cockpit of an AH-64 soon after Coalition forces liberated the Iraqi capital in early April 2003 (*CW2 Bill Neal*)

advancing troops for visual reconnaissance purposes, and then using them as aerial fire support for those troops in contact.

With the capture of BIAP, Apache units from the 11th AHR and 3rd AVN now had a FOB within the Iraqi capital itself that boasted relatively modern aviation facilities. From there, four AH-64 battalions were able to effectively stage missions which could reach almost anywhere in the US-controlled areas. By this point, attack aviation units maintained QRFs in order to respond as the ground situation developed, although they were not flying combat operations in the urban areas for safety reasons.

While the 3rd Infantry Division's armoured forces captured Baghdad with the brilliant 'Thunder Run', conducted by the division's mechanised infantry brigades, Apache units waited for a call to join the fray. Rob Purdy stood several QRF watches during this phase of OIF:

'Maj Gen Blount held all aviation west of the Euphrates until he knew what we were dealing with. He wanted no "Blackhawk Down" scenarios. As bad as we are, we cannot take the punishment that an M1 or a Bradley can. Urban environments are risky for attack aviation.'

In mid April, the 11th AHR was moved to Balad, roughly 50 miles north of Baghdad. As with the other attack units in Iraq, mid-month found the 2-6th and 6-6th Cavalry tasked with QRF duty, convoy escort and general area reconnaissance of their new AO.

'Palerider' pilots of B Troop, 6-6th Cavalry make the most of a rare break between sorties at the edge of LSA 'Anaconda's' airfield in April 2003 (*US Army*)

'Viper 14' of 1-3 AVN patrols over one of Saddam Hussein's former palaces during a reconnaissance-security mission on the outskirts of Baghdad in April 2003 (*CW3 Michael S Madura*)

The 101st Airborne's movement to Mosul in the closing days of the initial campaign further expanded the Apache's territory, allowing fire teams to roam virtually anywhere in-country at will in their efforts to cover Coalition ground forces whenever called upon.

On 1 May 2003, President George W Bush declared major combat in Iraq to be over. Although fighting continued throughout the country, organised resistance by the Iraqi military had come to a swift and decisive end. It was clear that while 'major' combat was over, actual combat was still a harsh and sudden reality that could flare up anywhere, at any time.

'VIPERS" WAR

As mentioned in the previous chapter, the 'Vipers' of the 1st Battalion (Attack), 3rd Aviation Regiment saw some of the first action of OIF when they attacked observation posts along the Kuwaiti–Iraqi border on 20 March 2003. Firing a single radar-frequency Longbow Hellfire missile – the first employed in anger – and 13 semi-active laser missiles, all of which obtained direct hits, the 'Vipers' had unleashed the first direct fire shots of the ground war. Hours later, 1-3 AVN also knocked out the first tank (a T-54) of OIF in the vicinity of Nasiriyah with a Longbow.

An eyewitness to the 'Vipers" war was Maj David Rude, who served as the battalion S-3 operations officer throughout OIF. For much of the campaign he resourced the fight from the ground in the 1st Battalion's Tactical Command Post (TAC). His battle staff's primary functions were to orchestrate the planning and execution of attack helicopter missions in concert with the intent of Aviation Brigade commander, Col Curtis Potts, and to integrate 1-3 AVN's assets into the overall fight in support of the 3rd Infantry Division (Mechanized). The TAC, which was co-located with the Aviation Brigade TAC, conducted location tracking of aircraft and units throughout the battlefield. It also provided the 18 AH-64D Longbow Apaches assigned to 1-3 AVN with a command and control node from the TAC on the ground, or from an airborne UH-60 Blackhawk command and control aircraft.

By 1 May 2003, 'Vipers" Longbow Apaches had flown a myriad of attack, reconnaissance and security missions, logging some 850 combat hours without a single loss to enemy fire. 'Viper' operations in OIF illustrate how this contemporary conflict revolutionised the way the AH-64 was used in combat. The unit fought alongside their mechanised and armour brethren during the quickest, most expeditionary attack across 400-plus miles of brutal desert combat in just 21 days – a first in the history of modern warfare.

In the first few days of the war the Longbow Apache was employed in much the same way as the Marine Corps were using their AH-1Ws – in close combat attacks (CCA) in support of ground forces. In the joint scheme of operations, units of the 3rd Infantry Division's Aviation Brigade and the 1st Marine Expeditionary Force operated in concert exceptionally well to manage airspace, share limited airfield resources and defeat the 11th Iraqi Infantry Division.

Lt Col Dan Williams ('Vipers' Battalion Commander), who led every battalion fight from the Longbow's cockpit, added:

'"Vipers" battalion's Longbows destroyed everything we were tasked to destroy, and much more besides, and we never dropped a single mission, including medical evacuation escort and no-notice QRF sorties in support of ground units.'

Incidentally, Lt Col Williams personally tested the combat reliability of the Longbow Apache during the very first AH-64 mission of the war.

A veteran Army Aviation pilot with over 1500 hours in his logbook, Maj David Rude was 1-3 AVN's battalion S-3 operations officer throughout OIF. Aside from flying the AH-64A/D, he has also piloted the UH-1, OH-58A/C and AH-1F since swapping howitzers for helicopters in 1989 (*Maj David Rude*)

59

Lt Col Dan Williams, commander of the 1st Battalion (Attack), 3rd Aviation Regiment during OIF, delivers a motivational speech to his troops at Camp Udairi, in Kuwait, on the eve of war. He provided command and control in the lead 1-3 AVN Longbow Apache on the crucial observation posts attack in the opening hours of OIF. During the mission execution, Williams' aircraft was hit by small-arms fire and forced down (it lost avionics, night vision and many other systems) in Iraqi territory. Williams made a hard landing into a sand dune, coming to rest on a 45-degree slope. Following a quick evaluation on the ground, and with enemy troops closing on their position, he and his co-pilot/gunner, CWO Dave Keshel, cranked the aircraft up and evacuated it safely back to Kuwait while the battalion completed its destruction of the target
(*CW3 Michael S Madura*)

While providing command and control for two attack helicopter companies engaging observation posts along the Kuwait–Iraqi border (see previous chapter for details) to launch the ground war, Williams' AH-64D (99-5125) was hit by a barrage of small-arms fire. The Apache, after losing night vision capability and avionics, landed hard at a 45-degree angle on the side of a large sand dune.

With enemy forces closing in on the downed machine, the crew conducted a hasty evaluation of their machine, which duly revealed no damage that would preclude further flight. Confident that his Apache was airworthy, pilot-in-command CWO Dave Keshel cranked the aircraft, levelled it gently for an unaided desert take-off and nursed the Apache safely back to Kuwait, while Williams reported his battalion's successful destruction of their targets. 99-5125 never missed a follow-on mission.

Maj Rude noted:

'The fight that raged around us in the opening days of the ground war was not at all like *Desert Storm*. Enemy air defences and AAA units had demonstrated adaptability and improvements in tactics, especially in their ability to target attack helicopters, since 1991. The enemy placed weapon systems beneath tree lines and palm canopies, and they tucked them into urban areas to exploit Apache vulnerabilities. On more than one occasion, the enemy employed an obviously lucrative target – often a T-55 or T-72 tank – in the open as bait, with the expectation of drawing Apaches into an air defence ambush. Near many ambush positions, observer teams in Arab civilian attire triangulated aircraft locations and directed mortar and AAA fires.

'The battlefield had changed as well. Our aviators flew into battle expecting to strike lucrative, high-payoff targets in the Iraqi corps and division deep battle space – mainly armour and artillery. After all, the Apache had proven itself against such targets in open desert combat 12 years earlier. In 2003, however, the Iraqis tucked their conventional weaponry inside city blocks, among family dwellings and behind human shields.

'To complicate the Apache's role in deep operations, tactical fighters performing the killbox interdiction close air support function on the battlefield often presented the ground commander with better options by mitigating tactical risk to aircrews through the circumvention of the enemy's air defence network.

'So why not aggressively bring Apaches back into the close fight during the 21st century? AH-1G HueyCobra gunships conducted close combat attacks (CCA) successfully in the Vietnam conflict, and more recently, Apaches in Afghanistan achieved success directly supporting ground troops. Even Marine Corps aviation units have firmly indoctrinated their AH-1W Super Cobra crews into "fighting the close fight" to support ground units in contact. The Army, on the other hand, has purposefully shunned the Apache's role in CCA for years.

'In addition, we have been taught to rely entirely too much upon intelligence-gathering systems that did not seem to help us visualise the enemy in Iraq. While conducting CCA against enemy forces who had pinned down a friendly ground convoy south-east of Nasiriyah, a Longbow Apache team from 1-3 AVN came under fire from ground mounted anti-tank (AT) weapons. The dismounted weapons were concealed along a road in a vehicular ambush position. They were transported by and set in close proximity to civilian pick-up trucks.

'After evading the direct fires of two AT missiles aimed at their aircraft, the hunter-killer team returned fire and destroyed four AT systems with a combination of semi-active laser K Model Hellfire missiles and 30 mm cannon fires. Suddenly, a large, conspicuous canvas-covered truck moved near the unfolding carnage. Without

warning, concealed troops in the back ripped away the canvas cover and sprayed small-arms fire at the aircraft, forcing the hunter-killer team to engage and destroy the truck and hostile troops.

'As in the vignette above, the enemy established ambush positions to hit our convoys moving north into zone. They used unconventional tactics "outside the box" to attack our weaknesses. It was difficult to determine who was friendly and who was not. Often, the enemy and civilians we faced were one and the same. The Iraqi soldiers were usually clad in civilian attire, not uniforms. For instance, as one Iraqi man standing atop a bridge raised his hands while holding up a white flag to surrender, there were others firing AT missiles at our helicopters from positions just a few metres away. It was a deliberate trap. These Iraqis were very cunning, and they employed guerrilla tactics against both our ground and airborne platforms. They were neither surrendering nor capitulating.

'The war rapidly shifted to fights against terrorists, and it slowly dragged us into guerrilla tactics not seen since Vietnam. There was no conventional, open desert fight as there had been in *Desert Storm*. Saddam had been using school buses, ambulances and other seemingly sacred vehicles to move troops and terrorists. He embedded command, control and communications nodes within schools, mosques and hospitals. He brutalised any Iraqis who showed support for Coalition efforts in Iraq.

'We were not fighting tanks in this war. Apaches were not sent after division artillery groups or large mechanised or armoured formations in engagement areas. The enemy was not arrayed as such. Instead, Saddam cultivated the fight close to his cities and forced our troops into urban warfare to instigate civilian and collateral damage with the intention of blaming us and swaying world opinion against us.

'Viper 17' sits on the ground at a hastily prepared FOB at Ramadi, west of Baghdad, in April 2003. Note the dirt berm, which has been created for use as an immovable wheel chock
(*CW3 Michael S Madura*)

'Viper 15' returns to an unidentified FOB in southern Iraq during the early stages of OIF
(*CW3 Michael S Madura*)

'Furthermore, gaps in intelligence coverage during OIF prevented us from attaining the real-time ability to track definitive enemy activity. Therefore, there were no enemy-driven decision points or triggers to launch Apaches to shape the indistinct battle space in front of ground commanders. UAVs were not available, and we simply did not have the means to detect, locate or track high-payoff target sets that would enable the commitment of our attack helicopter companies in a "Warfighter" maximum destruction attack at a decisive point. This is not, however, to be construed to mean that the Apache has no role, or is incapable of effective combat operations in such a battlefield environment.

'As the enemy's situation template became urban-centric instead of Soviet doctrine-based, with a conventional force in the open desert, the mission focus of 1-3 AVN transformed from massed battalion or phased attacks against armour and artillery, to continuous close combat attacks in support of the division's main effort BCT. During execution, the battalion routinely employed en route combat manoeuvres and close combat manoeuvres to enhance aircrew manoeuvrability and survivability through sustained running fire tactics, avoiding the infamous hover-fire trap from a targeted battle position.

'Due to the concentrated AAA and small arms threats all over the Iraqi battlefield, the battalion's aircraft always fought in teams, and we refrained from launching single Apaches on combat operations. The lead aircraft focused eyes and fires out to their point-target killing range, while wingmen provided local security for the team. The battalion commander, operating from an AH-64D, also provided local security behind the attack helicopter company in contact, and for the aviation brigade's command and control UH-60. Companies maintained back-up aircraft at the same readiness condition as the mission aircraft until the time of launch to preclude missing a mission.

'The battalion achieved notable success during the conflict with its newly-developed "ring of steel" tactic, which saw helicopters patrolling over key terrain to ensure that it was clear of enemy forces, before transitioning to close combat support for an advancing ground force. This concept centred upon a terrain-oriented objective, and the operation commenced with reconnaissance by fire to clear enemy direct fire weapon systems within a two-kilometre circle around the objective. AH-64s then shifted immediately to a four-kilometre circle around the objective to destroy enemy direct and indirect weapons systems. Once that area was cleared by AH-64s, responsibility for clearance of fires in the area shifted to the advancing ground task force commander. At that time, the Apaches focused reconnaissance and fires to an outer, eight-kilometre ring to protect the ground force.

'As an example of this concept in action, the battalion initially cleared the two inner circles around a bridge that was to be seized by a 3rd Brigade Combat Team armoured

Radar-equipped 'Viper 16' heads a line-up of three 1-3 AVN Apaches at Jalibah. All the helicopters boast the unit's distinctive sharksmouth marking (*CW3 Michael S Madura*)

task force. Once the task force closed to within their organic direct fire range of the bridge, the aircraft shifted to an outer security ring and focused their eyes on major avenues of approach to deny enemy counter-attack forces from affecting bridge-crossing operations.

'The fast-paced operational tempo required the battalion to be continually postured to launch an Apache company within a 30-minute window, from the start of the ground war through the duration of combat operations culminating in the seizure of BIAP. We maintained a standing "be prepared" mission to conduct security in support of contingency operations for the duration of the war. In addition, the battalion routinely provided security for medevac and casualty evacuation aircraft that transitioned between the front and ambulatory exchange points. We also supported downed aircraft recovery teams or immediate personnel recovery missions in support of the aviation brigade.

'For sustainability and depth, we maintained the next-up company on a two-hour launch string, while keeping the third company down for future contingencies. During operational missions in support of a BCT in contact, the battalion conducted continuous rotations of two attack helicopter companies for six- to eight-hour blocks to support the ground commander's fight against the Republican Guard Medina Division. Meanwhile, we retained the third company in a forward assembly area on

a reduced readiness condition that afforded aircrews an opportunity to rest. This third company provided the battalion the flexibility to conduct subsequent contingencies in support of the division.

'Whether in shaping the battle in a combined arms warfighter-type fight, where intelligence of the enemy is known, or by conducting close combat attacks in direct support of a ground commander, the Longbow Apache has shown in OIF I, II and III that it can provide significantly increased flexibility and firepower for US Army forces on the ground, and it will continue to do so for years to come.'

'Viper 04' carries a modified Hellfire load, whereby one of its M261 pods has been replaced by an external fuel tank. This configuration was adopted post-war, when mission duration rather than firepower became more important to 'Vipers' crews (*CW3 Michael S Madura*)

'Viper 02' heads out on yet another patrol in April 2003 (*CW3 Michael S Madura*)

END OF MAJOR COMBAT?

With the flourish of President Bush landing in an S-3B Viking aboard USS *Abraham Lincoln* (CVN-72), major combat in Iraq was declared over. Certainly, the invasion force had accomplished its initial goal of defeating the Iraqi military and removing Saddam Hussein from power, but declaring an end to hostilities proved to be premature. The invading army, originally received as a force of liberation, had by the summer taken on the role of occupier, with each division being given a tactical area of responsibility for which its commanding officer served as the region's de facto governor. Military control would remain in place until local governments could be established and self-rule handed over to the Iraqi people – a goal that US military commanders were all too eager to achieve.

By the cessation of major combat operations, an eighth Apache battalion (1-4th ATKHB) was available to Gen Tommy Franks. The 4th Infantry Division had initially been tasked with opening up a northern front in Iraq by invading across the Turkish border, but just days before OIF commenced, the Turkish parliament voted against letting the US force transit through its country. The entire division duly re-embarked onto their transport ships, which subsequently set sail for southern Iraq via the Suez Canal.

The effect of this unplanned detour was the fastest redeployment of a heavy division in history. Literally several hundred vehicles ranging in size from Humvees to M1A2 Abrams main battle tanks, dozens of helicopters and tons of soldiering equipment organic to the division was all offloaded in the Iraqi port city of Umm Qasr and moved northwards from mid-April onwards. The 1-4th ATKHB began flying its first screening patrols and column cover flights for the division vanguard soon after being offloaded onto Iraqi soil, before finally setting up a temporary operations HQ at BIAP on 18 April. Shortly afterwards, the 'Dragons' of the 1-4th AVN performed the unit's first combat missions in the Baghdad AO. Further south, the bulk of the 4th ID was still moving northwards towards the Iraqi capital.

It was the 'Dragons' that also saw the attack helicopter battalion's first

The maintenance wizards of the 1st Battalion, 4th Aviation reassemble an AH-64D at Umm Qasr soon after the unit's arrival in Iraq from Turkey in mid-April 2003 (*Capt John Tucker*)

These 'Sidewinders' Apaches from 1-4th ATKHB were photographed during C Company's short stay at BIAP in late April 2003 (*Capt John Tucker*)

action of the deployment at midnight on 1 May. Two AH-64Ds, serving in the QRF role, responded to one of the division's Shadow 200 UAVs which had observed insurgents, armed with AK-47s, loading stolen weapons and explosives into a truck at a storage facility near Saddam Hussein's hometown of Tikrit. A 1-4th fire team was quickly on the scene, and their intention was to cut off the insurgents' avenues of escape and force them to surrender to US troops on the ground. However, instead of giving up, the suspects foolishly attempted to raise their AK-47s and engage the hovering Apaches. They were outgunned by a deadly accurate burst of 30 mm cannon fire from one of the AH-64s that destroyed the insurgents' truck and killed all 14 occupants.

OPERATION *PENINSULA STRIKE*

In mid-May, the 4th Infantry Division's Task Force *Ironhorse* began its first major brigade-sized operation since the end to major combat had been declared two weeks earlier. Operation *Peninsula Strike* was instigated in an effort to quash the insurgents who were gaining in strength and increasing the frequency of their attacks north of Baghdad from their bases in the city of Tikrit.

4th Infantry Division AH-64Ds sit on newly built hardstanding at an undisclosed airfield in central Iraq in May 2003 (*USAF*)

The 'Dragons' of 1-4th AVN provided flawless overhead security for the infantry units undertaking the highly dangerous search operations in the towns most frequented by anti-Coalition forces. According to the unit's Capt John Tucker, C Company commander (call-sign 'Sidewinder 6'), 'It seemed like the better a job we did for the ground soldiers, the more often they wanted us to fly. They really valued us flying overhead while they performed the face-to-face work that needed to be done on the ground there. To a soldier on the ground,

65

the sight of a friendly attack helicopter flying overhead brings a great sense of security.'

That sense of security allowed the infantry to proceed at a more rapid pace than would have been the case had the Apaches not been overhead. As had been the case in Afghanistan during OEF, enemy forces simply did not show themselves when there were AH-64s in the area.

Concurrently, Bravo Company of the 'Reapers' was flying missions over Samarra, south of Tikrit, in search of suspected insurgents. Just as with C Company, the 'Reapers' were patrolling overhead while the infantry searched for weapons, documents or any other intelligence pertaining to the disposition of their elusive enemy. According to battalion commander Lt Col James Muskopf, 'Those Iraqis, who had previously been neutral to us at best, started telling the ground forces where all the ammunition caches and non-compliant Iraqis were. They then said "please do not send the helicopters back". Not a shot was fired, but the Apache itself was enough to make those people tell us what we needed to know to make their area safer.'

In June, Bravo Company of the 'Reapers' was sent to Mosul to provide air support for the 173rd Airborne Brigade. The 'Sky Soldiers' had tenuous control of the city, although as a light infantry unit they had very little in the way of vehicles or aircraft. The 'Reapers' duly provided the overhead security and reconnaissance that the 1000 paratroopers of the 173rd needed to maintain order, as well as take the fight to the insurgency.

Capt Scott Kruse's Bravo Company was also tasked with providing air support for the 173rd during the preliminary elections in Iraq, and to perform the QRF mission should the insurgency attempt to disrupt the election. He explained:

'We were sent to Mosul to help the 173rd bring peace to the restless city prior to the elections, which would establish a new local government. We supported ground brigades most of the time, and in the ten short days we operated over Mosul, we were able to see its transformation from a war torn city that had previously been controlled by Saddam Hussein, to a more open and peaceful conurbation. Our initial sorties over the city made for some interesting flying, as we regularly came into contact with the "not-so-friendly" elements based in Mosul. We handled these incidents in our stride, however.

'It was great to see the increasing level of trust gained by US forces in the city from the local populace in just a matter of days. Our flights became less intensive, and the locals became friendlier. The streets started filling with families again, street markets opened, soccer fields filled with children and schools reopened. It was a complete 180-degree turn around from our initial contact with the city, and it was good to play a part in that stabilisation. We also established some excellent working relationships with the ground forces.'

Coordinating air–ground cooperation is no easy task, as units often have difficulty in conducting realistic integration training, even if they come under the same command 'umbrella'. With their transfer to Mosul, the 'Reapers' were thrown into a situation where they were forced to coordinate with a unit that they had never trained with, and which was completely outside of their chain of command. Despite these difficulties,

Bravo Company was able to immediately agree SOPs with the ground commander, thus providing him with an immediate close combat attack capability when necessary. Capt Kruse concluded:

'After we had left Mosul, it was satisfying to hear that the 173rd Airborne Brigade's command HQ had reported to its counterpart in 4th ID that we had performed a superb job during our time there.'

COUNTERTERROR OPS

In the early hours of 12 June, a heavy fire team from A Company 'Renegades', 2-101st ATKHB joined coordinated air strikes by Coalition F-16s and AC-130s and a follow-up ground assault on a terrorist training facility in north-western Iraq, near the Syrian border. Operating under the cover of darkness, the Apache fire team moved in and attacked the target compound with cannon and rocket fire, although it in turn was opposed by accurate small-arms fire.

During the intense engagement, AH-64D 97-5039 was hit by AAA, bringing it down just outside the camp's perimeter. US forces immediately recovered the unharmed crew and secured the crash site, while the remaining two 'Renegades' Apaches continued supporting the ground elements that battled with the terrorists in the camp until the enemy threat was eliminated.

Although very little information has been released about this particular mission, it appears that the majority of US ground forces involved in the action were SOCOM units – most likely the 3rd Ranger Battalion. More than 80 enemy combatants were killed, while one US soldier was lightly wounded. The compound's armoury was filled with weapons intended for use against Coalition forces, including 70–80 SA-7s, roughly the same number of RPGs and numerous rifles and cases of small-arms ammunition.

Twenty-four hours after this engagement, B Company's 'Reapers' found their patience being tested by mechanical woes, rather than the enemy, as Capt Scott Kruse (call-sign 'Reaper 6') related:

'The "Reapers" were conducting their usual daylight reconnaissance mission with a two-ship flight. CW3 Scott Brodeur and I were flying one aircraft and CW2s Covington and Vaughn were in the other machine. That day, we'd happened to spot a local with a weapon coming out of a tree line, and CW3 Brodeur and I used our aircraft to stop him. We had him drop the weapon and stay where he was, while CW2s Covington and Vaughn directed the military police (MPs) to his location in order to apprehend him.

'Upon completion of this routine mission, and now low on fuel, we called "Bingo" and headed back to refuel. Just as CW3 Brodeur was getting the wings level to fly back home, CW2 Covington called "APU FIRE" over the radio and told us that he was putting his aircraft down on the ground. Due to us being in lead at the time, we didn't see them land, so we pulled a hard right turn and circled back to make sure that they had gotten down safely and successfully extricated themselves from the aircraft. By the time we had located them, the crew had already landed and evacuated the aircraft after completing an emergency shutdown.

'We called back to camp to report that we had a "downed bird", and that we needed a Maintenance Recovery Team (MRT). Once Covington and Vaughn had decided that there was no post-landing fire, they returned to the aircraft to see what the damage was, and then radio it back to us in the aircraft above. By then we'd established aerial security, called in ground security from the MPs and had the MRT en route.

'We were now very low on gas, so we called in two more B Company aircraft to provide over-watch by relieving us on station. Covington had reported that they had seen smoke in the cockpit, followed shortly after by the "APU FIRE" indication on the instrument panel.

A 1-4th Aviation AH-64D heads over downtown Baghdad on a post-war patrol. The gold dome of the Imam Ali mosque can be seen in the background (*Capt John Tucker*)

Following the MRT inspection on the AH-64, we learned that a drive shaft had separated from the transmission, causing the fire. Needless to say, Covington and Vaughn had done an excellent job getting the aircraft down in one piece and promptly extinguishing the fire. Their actions saved the Apache from total destruction. In fact we had the aircraft up and flying again within ten days.

'Once Brodeur and I had topped off our fuel tanks, our No 2 engine dumped all of its oil on restart, so that was the end of that aircraft for the day too! We quickly jumped into a second Apache and headed back out to replace the two other B Company helicopters that had replaced us on station. Of course, as soon as we'd done this our new machine gave us an "ENGINE CHIPS" light in the cockpit, which meant that we had to return immediately to base and shutdown. Meanwhile, one of the two aircraft which had replaced us for a second time had its computer system completely "freak out", so it too was down.

'So, with one aircraft in phase down for maintenance, a second down in the field following the APU fire, a third down with an engine oil leak, a fourth down for the "ENGINE CHIPS" light and a fifth down because its computer had gone unserviceable, we only had one aircraft left that was flyable. We also later learned that the Blackhawk that had flown in the MRT broke on our airfield due to mechanical failure! It was an unbelievable day. I had never seen so many aircraft go down like that for maintenance in just a matter of hours truly weird. B Company will never again fly on a Friday the 13th with a full moon.

'By the end of the day we had all of our aircraft and all of our soldiers safely recovered back to base. CW3 Auten and the crew chiefs worked double shifts that evening to ensure that we had all of our aircraft back up and flyable – except for the APU fire Apache and the one in phase – by the following morning.'

Auxiliary power unit fires, which had caused the first 'Reapers' AH-64 to make an emergency landing, continued to plague the Apache force in Iraq for the rest of the year. Indeed, on 30 October 2003 the crew of 6-6th Cav AH-64D 00-5211 made an emergency landing near Balad air base after they had an 'APU FIRE' warning light illuminate in the cockpit, quickly followed by 'ENG 1' and 'ENG 2' fire advisory lights. Their

'Sidewinders' C Company pilots and crews pose with one of their Apaches (*Capt John Tucker*)

wingman also confirmed that flames and smoke were coming from both engines. A controlled landing was made near Coalition forces and the crew safely exited the helicopter. The fire could not be extinguished, however, and the AH-64 was consumed by the conflagration.

This was the second Longbow Apache to be lost to an APU fire in a week, for on 23 October the crew of A Company, 2-101st AH-64D 00-5219 had carried out a forced landing at Kirkuk air base. The blaze was eventually extinguished by USAF firefighters, but not before it had caused the aircraft's back to break just forward of the tailboom.

An in-theatre investigation into both fires revealed that the forward-deployed 'bare-base' nature of operations, and the desert environment in which most FOBs were situated, had led to much greater reliance and longer running up times for AH-64 APUs compared to previous Army experience. Crash investigators concluded that this, together with the grease on the output duplex bearings within the APU suffering from the effects of the harsh environment, had resulted in a higher rate of APU failures. A 'new safety of flight' recommendation was issued by the Army that increased the frequency of APU inspections. This was accompanied by the despatching of special tool kits to Iraq to facilitate the proper disassembly and repacking of grease within the APU.

Returning to base after declaring an in-flight emergency and fire on 23 October 2003, 'Spectres' AH-64D 00-5219 from A Company, 1-101st Aviation was written off at Kirkuk air base after its fuselage burned completely through. The crew escaped unharmed (*USAF*)

Despite technical maladies having briefly rendered B Company of 1-227th AVN non-operational, *Peninsula Strike* continued, with brigades from the 4th Infantry Division searching along the banks of the Tigris River and through the town of Duluiyah, north of Baghdad. With so many 'Reapers' aircraft grounded, its two sister companies (the 'Vipers' and 'Sidewinders') worked overtime on 13 June, providing air cover for

cordon and search operations, as well as for convoys passing through the area.

1st ARMORED DIVISION

Shortly after the 4th Infantry Division set up operations in the Tikrit area and began flying around-the-clock combat missions, another Apache battalion arrived in-country when the 1st Armored Division deployed from Germany in late April to increase US troop strength in Iraq. With the arrival of the 'Flying Dragons' of the 1-501st AVN (not to be confused with the 1-4th 'Dragons', which had just arrived as well), Apache strength reached its peak at nine battalions in-theatre. This number would soon rapidly decrease, however, as both the 2-6th and 6-6th Cavalry would depart for Illesheim, Germany, in August.

Setting up shop at BIAP, which it used as its primary base for the next ten months, 1-501st crews quickly shook off their 'new guys' tag by rapidly establishing themselves as operators who provided first-class aerial fire support. As with other battalions in Iraq, the Apaches of the 1-501st were tasked out to whichever unit needed their support the most. That usually resulted in single companies being assigned to individual brigade combat teams within the division, although they could also be detached to fulfil other missions as the situation dictated.

1-501st Apache companies were duly assigned to 'hot spots' throughout the country as the tactical situation warranted, flying missions from bases as far south as Najaf and as far north as Mosul, and many locations in between. Since major ground units like the 82nd Airborne Division and 2nd Armored Cavalry regiment did not have their own organic AH-64 battalion, they relied on other major commands' Apaches for assistance as and when it was required.

DESERT SCORPION/IVY SERPENT

Following closely on the heels of Operation *Peninsula Strike*, *Desert Scorpion*, launched on 16 June, was specifically undertaken to find, fix and destroy Ba'athist elements in the central 'Sunni Triangle' region of Iraq, where most die-hard Saddam loyalists seemed to be originating from. Conducted primarily by the 4th Infantry Division, concurrent operations were also undertaken by the 1st Armored Division in the Baghdad AO and by the 101st Airborne Division in Mosul.

The 4th ID carried out several raids in Tikrit in the first 24 hours of the operation, utilising M1A2 Abrams tanks to break down the walls of certain targeted compounds. Overhead, AH-64D Longbow Apaches provided air cover while 4th ID infantrymen conducted house-to-house raids. In Fallujah, the division arrested eight suspected insurgent leaders during building searches supported by both 1-4th AVN's AH-64Ds and tanks. The troops raided homes and rounded up suspects, as well as confiscating numerous weapons, in an effort to stem the number of anti-American and anti-Iraqi attacks throughout the country. Further raids in June met with little success, however, and the insurgents escalated their ambushes on Coalition forces.

Following the disappointment of *Desert Scorpion*, the 4th ID changed its tactics with the commencement of Operation *Ivy Serpent* in late July. Instead of targeting specific individuals, this offensive was geared towards finding and removing weapons caches from the division's AO. Utilising combined arms task forces of infantry, armour and aviation, coupled with solid intelligence, these teams enjoyed significant success in capturing large arms caches that would have inevitably been used against US and new Iraqi government forces.

One major sensitive site exploitation was conducted by C Company, 3-66th Armor and C Company 1-22nd Infantry at a large home in Tikrit on 21 July. After an exhaustive search of the house and grounds that literally left no stone unturned, US soldiers discovered 225 AK-47 rifles, 42 crates of Composition B plastic explosive, 25,000 blasting caps and tens of thousands of rounds of 7.62 mm ammunition that had been earmarked for anti-US operations.

The following day, in one of the more peculiar moves of the war, 101st Airborne Division AH-64s were alerted, but never called upon, when infantry elements raided a house in Mosul. Light infantry units of the 3rd Brigade Combat (BCT), 101st Airborne attempted to enter a residence after getting solid intelligence that 'priority targeted' individuals were inside, but when they approached, a hail of AK-47 fire forced the 'door kickers' back. 101st AVN Apaches were immediately alerted and the QRF teams were placed on standby. A six-hour gun battle followed the initial contact, with ground units hitting the house with TOW missiles, 0.50-calibre machine-gun fire and countless 5.56 mm rounds.

OH-58D Kiowa Warriors from the 2nd Squadron, 17th Cavalry (the 101st's aerial reconnaissance unit) maintained two helicopters on-station throughout the entire battle, pouring round after round of 0.50-calibre fire into the building.

Curiously, the Apaches were never called upon to join the fight. Perhaps it was because the weaponry that they employ was determined to be too destructive in this case, and the overall mission commander wanted the opportunity to capture the occupants alive. Alternatively, perhaps the QRF helicopters had been called away on a different mission. Whatever the reason, the Apache force in Iraq was sidelined during the fight that killed Saddam Hussein's sons Uday and Qusay. This would not be the case when Saddam himself was captured five months later.

IRON HAMMER

The 1st Armored Division began its latest counterinsurgent operation on 12 November (codenamed *Iron Hammer*) with two separate actions against enemy forces. A 1-4th 'Dragons' fire team on patrol witnessed a civilian van launching mortar shells from an urban area in the Abu Ghraib district at around 2030 hrs local time. A ground QRF was despatched to intercept the vehicle, which remained under surveillance by the Apache team throughout. The van was observed relocating to several different firing positions, launching a few rounds, and then moving to another site. As soon as the vehicle had cleared residential areas, the 'Dragons' pounced, engaging the van with 30 mm cannon fire and quickly reducing it to little more than twisted wreckage.

When the ground QRF arrived on-scene to conduct an immediate Battle Damage Assessment, they found two insurgents dead and three wounded. The 1st AD soldiers captured an additional five fighters, as well as seizing documents, weapons and an 82 mm mortar tube.

A derelict SA 342L Gazelle formerly owned by the Iraqi Air Force is tried on for size by 1st Armored Apache pilots at an undisclosed base in central Iraq. Some 40 of these helicopters were supplied to the Iraqis in the early 1980s for use in the anti-tank role, and they saw much combat in the war with Iran (*Spc Antonio Allah*)

Throughout a week of 1 AD operations, 1-501st Apaches flew more than 20 specific attack missions, in addition to routine patrol and QRF duties. Crews coordinated their sorties with USAF AC-130s and A-10s, and also acted as forward observers for artillery fire missions. Operation *Iron Hammer* captured over 500 artillery and mortar rounds, 25 RPGs, four completed IEDs and two SA-7s. The operation also killed 14 insurgents and saw the capture of 104 others.

The ninth in a series of counterinsurgent operations conducted by the 4th ID's TF *Ironhorse* began during the second week of November with the launch of *Ivy Cyclone*, which saw attacks carried out on no fewer than 42 separate sites. These operations were aimed at denying the enemy use of his own territory and disrupting his sources of supply. In addition to targeting insurgent infrastructure, TF *Ironhorse* conducted six raids in which 4th ID soldiers captured 36 individuals suspected of being insurgents themselves, or assisting the insurgency in some way.

As a somewhat mundane, but essential part of these counterinsurgent operations, 'Dragons' AH-64Ds targeted an athletics field in Samarra that was a known mortar firing point in order to deny further use of that position, and also to create confusion during raids in the vicinity. Several other sites were also hit by 'Dragons' rocket fire due to their proximity to Allied installations, and their potential for use in attacks against them.

This series of operations in the months following the official ending of major combat on 1 May 2003 revealed that there was still plenty of fight left in the anti-Coalition insurgents (whose ranks had been significantly boosted by an influx of foreign fighters) scattered throughout Iraq. This had hardly been the case during the previous six weeks, when OIF forces had completed a stunning combined arms advance north from Kuwait.

But the actual seizing of the country soon proved to be the least of the problems facing the Bush administration, which had seemingly failed to effectively address the larger strategic issue of 'now that we have it, what do we do with it?' The end result of this failure has been the escalation of the conflict in Iraq into a much more dangerous and costly venture than could ever have been envisaged in Washington, DC, and where ten times the number of American lives have been lost since the official cessation of major combat.

COUNTER -INSURGENCY

Following an escalation in roadside and suicide bombings and insurgent mortar and RPG attacks on US and Iraqi government interests in the second half of 2003, Apache units were increasingly tasked with flying close support missions. These were more reminiscent of the convoy escort and aerial reconnaissance sorties undertaken by the AH-1 Cobra in Vietnam than the high-speed, high-threat environment in which the AH-64D was designed to fight. Working in

conjunction with convoys operating throughout Iraq, Apache units quickly adapted to the new environment and combat conditions, altering their weapons and fuel loads to adapt to the evolving threats. Often, only two Hellfire missiles would be carried, since armoured targets were rarely encountered. Crews instead chose a mixture of different rocket types and full cannon loads, retaining a few Hellfires to handle situations where pinpoint accuracy was needed.

Although tensions were always high during combat missions in Iraq, by the autumn and winter of 2003 Apache crews were rarely taking direct fire, and it was an even rarer occasion when they were free to roam the battlefield and hit targets of opportunity, as had been the case during the initial invasion. A distinct pattern had by now emerged for AH-64 units

1-501st AVN AH-64A 87-0444 was photographed between patrols at a FARP near Al Kut, south-east of Baghdad, in late 2003 (*Spc Antonio Allah*)

Performing the same column cover duties that their fathers and grandfathers may have performed in Vietnam or World War 2, an Apache crew from 1-501st AVN provides over-the-horizon reconnaissance for a US Army vehicle convoy in 'bandit country' north of Baghdad in November 2003 (*Spc Antonio Allah*)

in-theatre, with combat operations primarily consisting of cordon and search sorties in support of troops looking for weapons caches, key Ba'athist regime personalities and intelligence on the insurgency.

One such mission was Operation *Bulldog Mammoth*, which targeted Abu Ghraib on 10 December 2003. While the 1st Armored Division's 3rd BCT conducted a massive search of nearly 3000 apartments and other buildings, a platoon of AH-64s from the 'Steel Hunters' of C Company, 1-501st AVN,

provided aerial security and on-call fire support for the five-hour operation. No shots were fired, or taken, during the mission, but a great deal of insurgent equipment was discovered and confiscated during the search. In all, the 3rd BCT seized 220 AK-47 assault rifles and other small arms, 24 body armour inserts and a US-made vest, 16 cases of Meals Ready to Eat (MREs), 12 mortar sights, ten hand grenades, 15 RPG launchers with five rockets, an assortment of bomb-making materials, Russian-made night vision goggles, chemical protective masks and Saddam Hussein propaganda. At the conclusion of the mission, more than 40 suspected insurgents and collaborators were in US custody.

Successful missions like *Bulldog Mammoth* continued on a near-daily basis, with Apache battalions from the 1st Armored, 4th Infantry and 101st Airborne flying near-constant missions in support of ground operations. While certainly not as glamorous as the battlefield-shaping deep-attack missions for which the Apache was originally intended, the security umbrella that AH-64 units provided to ground units on patrol was immeasurable. Insurgents quickly gained a respect for the Apache's devastating firepower, and soon learned that they would live longer if they chose to attack American convoys and patrols when Apaches were not providing security overwatch.

Although *Bulldog Mammoth* was a good news story for the attack helicopter community on 10 December, an incident near Mosul that same day served as a stark counterpoise. Yet another Apache was lost to a suspected mechanical failure when a 101st AVN AH-64D came down near a highway about 15 miles south of the Iraqi city. Local witnesses to the incident said that they believed the Apache had been shot down whilst on a low-level patrol of the area. However, the crew, who had escaped without injury, later stated that they had noticed smoke, and heard a grinding noise, coming from the transmission area. The 'No 2 ENG TRANSMISSION' caution light then illuminated in the cockpit, and after an emergency landing and shut down, the 'AFT DECK FIRE' light came on. The AH-64 was burnt out in the subsequent blaze.

OPERATION *RED DAWN*

Working in conjunction with the 4th Infantry Division's 'Raider' Brigade and SOF Task Force '121', both of which were assigned to hunt down former Ba'athist leaders, 1-4th Aviation provided aerial security for the overall operation. Over 600 soldiers converged on a farmhouse within an orange grove in Ad Dawr, outside of Tikrit, in the early evening of 13 December 2003. They had been here twice before looking for key members in Saddam's regime, but both times they had come up empty-handed. 'Dragons' Apache crews kept a careful watch of the surrounding area through their TADS/PNVS-mounted FLIR sensors to ensure that any attempts to escape by the locals would be strongly discouraged.

Of particular concern was the ease with which someone trying to escape the orange grove could reach the banks of the Tigris River and swim to freedom. Because of this, a 'Dragons' fire team was specifically tasked with observing the riverbanks to make sure that no one got out. The ground elements were expecting a major firefight like the one in Mosul five months earlier that had ended in the deaths of both of Saddam's sons, so they approached swiftly, infiltrating the compound before the occupants knew they were under attack. Two men were detained, but they offered little information as to the whereabouts of the High Value Target that was supposed to be hiding there. But keen observation by SOF operators revealed a hidden bolt hole in the ground within the farm's courtyard, from which Saddam Hussein would be pulled moments later.

Although they did not fire a shot during the raid, 'Dragons' AH-64 crews played an essential role in the operation, providing security for the raid and, if necessary, immediate fire support for the ground commander should he have needed it in order to eliminate any threat emanating from the compound. The entire raid lasted only 30 minutes

Following Saddam Hussein's capture, it was expected that insurgent operations throughout Iraq would lessen. In retrospect, it has become apparent that Saddam had little or no direct control of these attacks, and was simply hiding in a hole, hoping the Americans would not find him.

US operations continued throughout the country, and five days later the 4th Division's 3rd BCT launched Operation *Ivy Blizzard* into the city of Samarra. According to brigade and operational commander Col Frederick Rudisheim, 'The overwhelming majority of Samarrans were fed up with the Saddam Fedayeen and terrorists carrying out their attacks.'

As with other brigade-sized raids, the Apache company attached for aerial support was utilised in several simultaneous capacities. The 'Sidewinders' of C Company were able to direct patrols by employing the Pilot's Night Vision System (PNVS), and they were also on-station to provide overwhelming fire support as needed. The operation's key objective was to isolate and destroy insurgent cells within the city of Samarra. Numerous weapons caches were captured during the sweep, which included a number of shoulder-fired SA-7 and HN-5 SAMs.

Phase II of *Ivy Blizzard* commenced on 19 December, with massive building reconstruction forming the focus of this aspect of the operation. With the 3rd BCT's presence in Samarra, insurgents were less likely to interfere with the creation of a new infrastructure for the Iraqi people in the city. Three million US dollars were allocated for the rebuilding process in Samarra by the 3rd BCT, Coalition military efforts focusing more on reconstruction rather than combat during this period.

With the situation in Samarra now seemingly under control, US forces turned their attention to Baghdad itself, and specifically the southern suburbs of the Iraqi capital. The dawning of Christmas Day saw an overwhelming combined arms assault hit these areas, with Apaches, supported by at least a dozen artillery rounds and AC-130s, targeting numerous known insurgent havens throughout the Al Doura district. The entire 1st Battalion, 501st AVN, plus two troops of Apaches from the 4th Squadron, 3rd Armored Cavalry Regiment (ACR) participated in the operation, utilising their Apaches' TADS/PNVS sensors to acquire and track targets for the division in the pre-dawn darkness.

This operation was the first to utilise intelligence gleaned from Saddam Hussein's debriefing to pinpoint several former Ba'athist strongholds in the city. Due to the source of the information, the entire division was committed to the operation, with one company from the 1-501st AVN supporting each of the three manoeuvre brigades and the air cavalry

This Q Troop, 4-3 ACR AH-64A was struck by a shoulder-launched SA-7 SAM on 21 January 2004 while flying convoy protection in the 'Sunni Triangle'. Although it lost an engine, the helicopter was successfully force-landed by its crew (*via John Musick*)

Positioned in trail behind his fire team leader, a 4-3 ACR AH-64 pilot looks out from his cockpit towards the Euphrates River ahead of him (*via John Musick*)

troops being attached to the ground cavalry units. This one-day offensive achieved the desired results, at least in the short term, as insurgent activity in the Al Doura district was significantly reduced over the coming months.

The same could not be said for the area around Falluja, however, for at 0930 hrs on 13 January 2004, 4-3 ACR had one of its AH-64As downed by AAA. The helicopter crash-landed in a dirt field ten miles north of Habbaniyah and 12 miles west of Falluja itself, both crew members escaping from their machine uninjured. The Apache had been performing an aerial security patrol for a ground convoy transiting through the area when it was hit. The helicopter was later recovered for possible repair.

LUCKY FIND

As a response to the increasing number of roadside bombs employed by the insurgency, the 4th Infantry Division began Operation *Trailblazer* to seek out these improvised explosive devices (IEDs) and destroy them before they could be used against US forces. The mission's objective was to maintain safe roadways through the 4th ID's TAOR, and eliminate any insurgents and IEDs found along them. 'Dragons' Apaches figured heavily in this operation, assisting with locating, marking and, in some cases, destroying roadside bombs with M230 cannon fire.

Initiated in the last week of January 2004, the operation met with a great deal of success, using 'Dragons' AH-64s to conduct reconnaissance ahead of the advancing armoured sweeps in search of IEDs. During one such sortie on 27 January, Apaches from A Company located seven operational ZPU-57-2 anti-aircraft guns south of Ash Sharqat, near Tikrit. Although unmanned, the presence of functional AAA batteries in the area was determined to pose a significant threat to both air and ground operations. The 'Dragons' fire team was ordered to destroy all seven gun systems, and they duly did so using 30 mm cannon fire.

On 2 February, 'Dragons' Apaches were again operating with elements of the 1st Battalion, 22nd Infantry when the fire team, ranging ahead of the advancing troops, spotted a suspicious site that could have been a weapons cache. The Apache crews called in soldiers on the ground to investigate while they provided overhead security. The troops quickly uncovered 200-plus 100 mm artillery shells that had gone undiscovered during the initial invasion of Iraq. Combat engineers were then brought in to mark the site and blow the cache up in situ.

February 2004 also saw the last combat missions flown by the 101st Aviation Brigade's three Apache battalions. The division began preparing for redeployment to Fort

Bearing a distinctive 'Q' on its engine exhaust fairing, this Q Troop, 4-3 ACR AH-64A was photographed conducting a rare patrol over the featureless desert in western Iraq (*via John Musick*)

Campbell in January, and started rotating its subordinate units home during the first days of the following month. Task Force *Olympia*, built around the 2nd Infantry Division's 3rd BCT, began arriving in Mosul in late January to replace the 101st. The transfer of control was completed by 20 February.

With the 101st Aviation Brigade rotating home, the attack helicopter presence in northern Iraq shrank considerably. Task Force *Olympia* arrived in-theatre without an Apache battalion under its control, and it was not until the late summer that the South Carolina Army National Guard's 1-151st AVN deployed to Iraq. Because of this, the centrally-based 1-501st and 1-4th AVNs were forced to readjust their areas of operation to provide additional coverage for units conducting missions in Mosul, Kirkuk and As Suleimaniyah.

APACHES FOIL IED ATTACK

The near omnipresence of unmanned aerial vehicles over the battlefield had greatly affected the counter-insurgency operations being conducted in Iraq by early 2004. Army Shadow 200 Tactical Unmanned Aerial Vehicles (TUAVs), flying thousands of feet overhead, provided real-time battlefield intelligence that commanders could utilise to best exploit a combat situation without being detected. TUAVs also improved response times for Apache units called on to deal with developing combat situations by keeping alert aircrews sharper, as well as saving fuel and reducing wear on the AH-64s themselves by decreasing the number of manned patrols required. Once a TUAV unit reported enemy activity, an Apache QRF could then be vectored directly into the target area.

Featuring a newly applied 'sharksmouth', this 4-3 ACR AH-64A carries the now-standard mission load-out of one IR Hellfire and two rocket pods per stub wing (*via John Musick*)

An Army TUAV proved its worth on 4 March when it observed six individuals acting suspiciously alongside a road leading to the town of Zaghiriyah. It was quickly determined that these men were planting IEDs, so a 1-4th AVN QRF was despatched to the site. In the ensuing engagement, the crew killed at least one of the insurgents, and wounded several others, with 30 mm cannon fire. The Apache fire team then broke contact to allow further surveillance of two suspects

Soon to head out on patrol, a 4-3 ACR crew settle into their cockpits prior to starting up their Apache (*via John Musick*)

who had retreated into the town. When the insurgents attempted to recover their dead and wounded a short time later, an AC-130H was called in to disrupt them further by firing a single 105 mm howitzer round into their midst.

Meanwhile, soldiers from Task Force '3-67 Armor' were tasked with conducting a raid on the building into which the survivors had retreated. Storming the dwelling moments after the insurgents had returned, they captured five men, three of whom were wounded. The latter were transferred to Baqubah hospital, while the others were taken into Iraqi police custody, completing a successful combined arms mission, and potentially saving numerous American and Iraqi lives.

This action was one of the last involving AH-64s from the 1-4th Aviation Battalion, as it began to wind down its operations at FOB 'Speicher' just days later following the arrival of the first 'Gunfighters' units from 1-1st AVN, based in Ansbach, Germany. The new battalion immediately began flying missions from both FOB 'Speicher' (A and B Companies) and LSA 'Anaconda' (C Company), at Balad, accumulating 750-plus combat hours in just three weeks. By comparison, in a normal year in Germany, each company would fly roughly 1500 hours in total!

The 1st Infantry Division took full control of the 4th Division's TAOR on 13 March 2004, extending divisional control over three Iraqi provinces, including the infamous 'Sunni Triangle', where a large percentage of insurgent attacks have occurred. The 'Gunfighters' were immediately thrown into combat operations, coming to the aid of their own maintenance and Headquarters & Headquarters Company convoy that had come under attack along the highway north of Baghdad as they drove to their new home at FOB 'Speicher' from Kuwait. The 'Gunfighters' were awarded a Valorous Unit Citation for their actions in response to this ambush.

Initially, supply convoys were having a difficult time getting north to 'Speicher' along the 'highway of death'. Insurgent attacks on unarmoured vehicles such as supply trucks had slowed the MSR (Main Supply Route) to a trickle. Because of this, the dining facilities at FOB 'Speicher', LSA 'Anaconda' and other central-Iraqi FOBs were short on food, forcing soldiers to regularly eat MREs.

In an effort to eradicate this threat, and ensure that the MSR remained open to all vehicles, and not just tanks and APCs, 'Gunfighters' Apaches were specifically tasked with convoy support along the main artery from Baghdad northwards. After a few weeks of engaging insurgents ahead of the approaching convoys, the supply situation quickly improved, along with the food! As most units operating in Iraq found during their tenure in-country, when the Apaches were overhead, the chances of them being attacked were slim.

Maintenance crews work on a 'Ghostriders' AH-64A from B Company, 1-1 AVN at Irbil in late 2004. Deployed from Ansbach, Germany, the 1-1st relieved 1-4th AVN at FOB 'Speicher' in March 2004. Groundcrews generally found that their Apaches coped well with the austere frontline operations of OIF. From a serviceability standpoint, their greatest enemy was the talc-like sand that proliferated in southern and western Iraq. It prematurely eroded rotor blades and had a habit of getting into the Apache's fuel system. Aircraft also proved more susceptible to unserviceability *after* major servicing, as their internals were often exposed to the elements for extended periods of time during 250-hour phase maintenance (*US Army*)

With 1-1st AVN's C Company being located at a separate base from the remainder of the battalion, it operated semi-autonomously from LSA 'Anaconda'. The 'Ghostriders', led by Capt Lee Fennema, forged close links with the division's 2nd and 3rd BCTs in the Samarra, Tikrit and Baqubah areas for the company's first two months in Iraq, supporting convoy and cordon and search operations, along with acting as a QRF for the supported brigades. With the 101st now back in the US, the 'Ghostriders' were also called upon in May to provide air support to then 'Apacheless' 1st Brigade, 25th Infantry Division in the Kirkuk area while the brigade conducted operations.

C Company had completed its flying with the 25th ID by early June, and with 1-1st AVN's 'Taz Devils' and 'Wolfpack' AH-64s busy participating in division operations from FOB 'Speicher', the 'Ghostriders' were reassigned to cover the 2nd Armored Cavalry Regiment (ACR) as it prepared for its redeployment home to Fort Polk, Louisiana. This effectively meant a great deal of column cover flying for the Apache crews, who conducted overhead security and reconnaissance missions for the rest of the month.

With the 2nd ACR based in the southern part of Iraq near Najaf and the ancient ruins of Babylon, the 'Ghostriders' got the chance to operate in a completely different AO. The incoming units to the Najaf AO were US Marine Corps assets, and for a brief time Army Apaches and Marine Corps AH-1W Super Cobras flew side-by-side in-theatre, protecting troop movements on the ground.

The 1st Armored Division also began scaling back its operations in Iraq in June, and with its 1-501st AVN scheduled to redeploy to Fort Hood for AH-64D conversion training immediately upon its return to Germany, the battalion was allowed to leave its now surplus AH-64As in Iraq for other units to utilise. This move proved particularly fortuitous for the 'Gunfighters'' SFC Jason Bryant:

'Around 12 July the battalion was given a special mission – to fly our crippled pup of an aircraft [AH-64A 87-0475] to BIAP to exchange it for a better 1-501st AVN bird. During our stay at the airport, we inventoried all of the necessary equipment, signed for the aircraft and launched a mission with our "new" helicopters manned by 1-501st AVN pilots. Later that day, the seven ex-1-501st AVN helicopters left BIAP with Lt Col David Moore [call-sign "Gun 6"] leading the way in an AH-64 that had no air-conditioning!'

Of the seven Apaches that the 'Gunfighters' absorbed, three went to B Company (one to replace the ailing 87-0475) and two each to A and C

A Company, 1-227th ATKHB Lot 7 AH-64D 02-5289, complete with rare tail art (see above), is prepared for another mission by its groundcrew at LSA 'Anaconda', in Balad (*Scott Brown and CW2 John Rawls*)

Companies, bringing each company up to an overstrength level of eight AH-64As apiece. Considering the operational tempo set by the battalion, where each company was sometimes flying upwards of 1000 hours a month, the new aircraft were a welcome addition. However, their arrival significantly increased the maintenance crews' workload

By mid-July the 'Ghostriders' had returned north to support 25th ID operations around Kirkuk, and they remained here until September, when the company was notified of its impending move to join the remainder of the battalion at FOB 'Speicher' in September.

OIF RECORD

The 'Gunfighters' battalion's record in Iraq in 2004 was an impressive one, as the following deployment summary by its CO, Lt Col David Moore, reveals:

'1-1st AVN conducted continuous 24-hour combat operations over a period of 210 days. The battalion flew nearly 8000 combat hours on 944 missions, with a 98 per cent mission success rate. The battalion never turned down a mission, and was only forced to abort 16 times due to maintenance. Hasty and deliberate attacks destroyed anti-Iraqi forces and equipment, including snipers, vehicles, boats, ammunition caches, heavy calibre and anti-aircraft weapons, IEDs and supplies. During the battalion's time in Iraq, there were no accidents, deaths or major injuries.'

Only eight 'Gunfighters' Apaches suffered battle damage throughout the entire time the battalion was in combat, and all were returned to flight status within 24 hours. One AH-64 also force-landed with mechanical problems near Balad on 16 July 2004, although its crew escaped injury. A downed Aircraft Recovery Team was despatched from FOB 'Speicher' in a 2-1 AVN UH-60, escorted by a 1-1 AVN Apache, and they quickly deemed the helicopter to be unflyable. The recovery team had the AH-64's rotor blades removed within an hour, and a specially designed new sling set known as a U-MARK (improved, utility, multi-purpose aircraft recovery kit) was attached.

Created in such a way that it can be used for the recovery of all types of US Army helicopter currently in the inventory, the U-MARK allowed the Apache to be slung beneath a CH-47D, which in turn carried it to LSA 'Anaconda'. Following a brief examination, the AH-64 was transferred to a repair facility for rectification work to be carried out by 1-1 AVN's hard-worked maintenance crews.

The 'Gunfighter' groundcrews played a major part in allowing the unit to sustain around-the-clock operations, as they successfully integrated Apache phase maintenance (each airframe had to be inspected after 250 flying hours) into the unit's hectic mission schedule. The 1-1st AVN 'Vikings' Maintenance Company was given a maintenance schedule three to four times more intense than peacetime operations, and with an additional company's worth of aircraft to maintain. Yet they kept a constant readiness rate of 80 per cent for all battalion helicopters, which for the most part were 1987-model AH-64As. Their efforts allowed the battalion to achieve a staggering 98 per cent mission success rate.

As a direct result of its achievements during OIF II, the 'Gunfighters' were nominated for the 2004 Combat Arms Lt Gen Ellis D Parker Award, presented to the top combat aviation unit in the Army.

CW2 Francis of the 'Death Dealers' B/1-501st AVN prepares for another mission from Balad in support of 1st Armored Division operations (*US Army*)

ONGOING OPERATIONS

Almost two years after major combat was declared over, Apache units in Iraq, like their counterparts in Afghanistan, are still engaging terrorist insurgents on a daily basis. As this volume goes to press, there are currently three battalions serving in Iraq and companies from two ARNG battalions in Afghanistan. Tasked with convoy escort, reconnaissance, airfield security and close air support, Apache units have maintained the highest operational readiness rates and have never turned down a mission.

As unit rotations have continued, the ARNG has been called on to meet necessary troop strength requirements and various missions in both theatres of operation. The attack aviation community is no different in this respect, and currently, the Florida, South Carolina and Utah ARNGs have deployed companies from their respective AH-64 battalions to Afghanistan and Iraq.

As the conflict continues, more Guard attack units will be called upon to perform this essential mission of providing air cover and advanced warning for Active Duty and ARNG troops on the ground, along with the necessary firepower to insure that when those troops are engaged by the enemy, they will have the airborne assets necessary to come out on top.

HEAVY FIGHTING

April 2004 saw heavy fighting in the western Baghdad district of Sadr City. The catalyst for this uprising in the Iraqi capital's poorest district was the attempted apprehension of Shia cleric Moqtada al-Sadr by US authorities in connection with the murder of a rival cleric. As Coalition forces moved into the area, they met with stiff opposition from al-Sadr loyalists hell bent on resisting the 'American Occupiers'.

Apaches of the 1st Battalion, 227th AVN flew numerous sorties in support of 1st Cavalry troopers and US Marines on the ground as they entered Sadr City, assisting in cordon and search operations and providing pinpoint aerial artillery when called on.

At 1030 hrs on 11 April, CW3 Chuck Fortenberry and CW2 Shane Colton from C Company

Spc Matthew White from A Company, 615th Aviation Regiment, 4th Brigade Combat Team, 1st Cavalry Division stands beside an AH-64D Apache Longbow preparing to lift off for a maintenance check flight near Baghdad on 16 December 2004 (*US Army*)

were flying just such a mission when they received an urgent request for air support on the emergency radio net. An American fuel convoy had come under attack in the Abu Ghraib district of Baghdad, three miles from BIAP. Having already suffered several casualties, the soldiers were now fighting for their lives as the insurgents threatened to overrun their position. Reaching the convoy within minutes, Fortenberry and Colton immediately engaged the enemy forces, thus allowing the US troops to break contact and escape. During the course of the firefight, the Apache was brought down by a SAM (almost certainly an SA-7) strike, which knocked out an engine and destroyed several rotor blades. Neither crewman survived the crash.

Increasing threats from the Sadr City district of Baghdad warranted increased Apache patrols over the city in support of 1st Cavalry troops sweeping the area in Ausgust 2004. Here, a 1-1 AVN AH-64 covers a heavily armed and armoured Humvee fitted with an M240B and a MK19 automatic grenade launcher (*US Army*)

In true testament to the AH-64 efficacy as a close air support platform, Sgt Maj James Ross, who was the senior enlisted man on the ground that day, made the following comment on Fortenberry and Colton's actions on 11 April in the US Army's *First Team* newsletter:

'We were heavily engaged by 20 or so insurgents and were getting down to the last of our ammunition. We knew that without air support, we would not be able to secure the convoy and evacuate the wounded. We called in for "air", and those Apaches showed up about 15 minutes later. Every trooper cheered, as they enabled us to get to a safe location. We then watched in horrified amazement as the Apache was shot down. Thank you for all that you and your pilots do in support of troops on the ground.'

The tenacity with which Fortenberry and Colton had engaged the enemy, along with their ultimate sacrifice, set the tone for 'First Attack' missions throughout the remainder of the unit's tour, which came to an end in the early spring of 2005.

Although April 2004 was the 1st Cavalry Division's most intense month of combat in its 12-month tour of duty, the unit's Apaches were kept busy around the clock throughout the summer and autumn too, providing a rapid and flexible armed response for Coalition troops engaged on the ground. These operations included supporting forces involved in the siege of the Imam Ali shrine in Najaf in August, when Mehdi Army militiamen loyal to Moqtada al-Sadr occupied holy sites in the city for almost a month. Further fighting in Sadr City also took place at around this time, stretching AH-64 resources in-country.

DARING RESCUE

On 16 October, while on a routine night reconnaissance patrol south of Baghdad, Capt Ryan Welch and his back seater, CW2 Justin Taylor, received a distress call on the Guard frequency telling them that two US helicopters had gone down in their vicinity. Immediately vectoring to the crash site, Welch and Taylor set their AH-64D (02-5300) down to assess the situation.

Two OH-58Ds from 1-25th AVN had collided during a night mission and crashed in an open field south-west of BIAP. The crew of one of the Kiowa Warriors (Capt Christopher Johnson and CWO William Brennan) had been killed outright in the collision, but CWOs Chad Beck and Greg Crowe were extracted from the wreckage of their helicopter severely injured, but alive. They needed to be medevaced out immediately, and according to Capt Welch, 'They were both in the early stages of shock, with their eyes glazing over and their faces bleeding profusely.'

Welch was able to get Beck to assist him in moving Crowe to the front seat of his Apache. He then helped Beck attach his AIRSAVE survival harness to the exterior of the AH-64D, and following suit, moved around to the other side of the aircraft and secured himself to it. Taylor added power and took off with both Beck and Welch secured to the outside of the aircraft. The four pilots then flew 20 kilometres to the nearest field hospital to allow the two injured men to get the medical attention they urgently required.

The following month, the majority of the AH-64s in Iraq were committed to the large-scale offensive to retake Falluja, codenamed Operation *Al Fajr* ('New Dawn'). The renewed fighting in the troubled city west of Baghdad was the end result of increased insurgent attacks on Iraqi police stations and government politicians. Launched on 8 November 2004, *Al Fajr* saw two battalions of the 1st Cavalry Division and four from the 1st Marine Division push into Falluja in an effort to eliminate terrorist groups based there. Clearing the city of insurgents on a house-by-house and street-by-street basis, the troops on the ground were supported throughout the bloody battle by Apaches from the 1-1st Avn and the 1-227th AVN. Both units provided overhead security for potentially vulnerable vehicle convoys moving soldiers and supplies in and around the city, as well as engaging in numerous CAS missions for Army and Marine troops in direct contact with the insurgents.

An indication of just how fierce the fighting was in the Falluja area can be gauged by the level of damage inflicted on US helicopter units committed to *Al Fajr*. On 10 November two Marine AH-1Ws were downed by RPGs, followed three days later by a UH-60, which was hit by AAA near Taji. A pair of AH-64s were struck by small-arms fire near the village of Zaidan, south-east of Falluja, on the 12th, although both crews managed to fly their helicopters back to BIAP. Finally, 24 hours later, two Army OH-58Ds were badly shot up by insurgents firing machine guns and RPGs in an ambush near Karma, north-east of Falluja.

EMBASSY ESCORT

Aside from their participation in headline-grabbing offensives such as *Al Fajr*, Army attack units continue to perform a multitude of more mundane, but nevertheless important, missions throughout Iraq on a daily basis. One of the Apache's more unusual taskings which provides a break from the norm is escorting VIP-laden UH-60s from the US embassy in Baghdad to various locations across the country. Presently, whenever high-ranking dignitaries are transported by helicopter, an Apache fire team escort is despatched from either 1-1 or 1-227 AVNs to protect the two embassy detachment UH-60s, flown by B Company,

Capt Ryan Welch (left) and CW2 Justin Taylor undertook a daring rescue mission that saved the lives of two fellow Army aviators on 16 October 2004. Capt Welch 'self-extracted' after placing an injured Kiowa crewman in his seat and securing the other Kiowa crewman to the opposite side of the helicopter. He then hooked himself to the outside of his Apache and CW2 Taylor took off and headed for the nearest field hospital (*US Army*)

1-171 AVN. While it is rare that these flights are ever engaged by enemy forces due to the presence of Apache escorts, these missions do give the overworked attack pilots a welcome change of scenery from their usual AO.

CW2 John Rawls, who completed a tour flying one of the embassy's UH-60s in 2003-04, flew with Apache escorts on several occasions:

'Whenever we had the ambassador or a general of three stars or higher aboard, we were escorted by the AH-64s. On one occasion, we were carrying British Foreign Secretary Jack Straw from Baghdad to Ducant, located in north-west Iraq. Two Longbow Apaches from the 227th Attack were attached to us for the day, meeting us early at the embassy heliport. We arrived at our destination in Ducant and landed in the parking lot of a resort on Lake Docan, where the British foreign minister was to meet with Kurdish officials. While we were there, our Kurdish hosts laid out a veritable feast for us, and this proved to be a real treat for the Apache crews who had been eating in the same chow hall for months on end!

'After eating a meal fit for a king, we mounted up late in the day and headed south for our first fuel stop in Kirkuk. About ten minutes out from the refuelling point, our "Chalk 2" Blackhawk suffered a bird strike that blew out the co-pilot's chin bubble. We all landed safely there, but the second Hawk couldn't continue on safely, so all of the VIPs were loaded into our helicopter and we returned safely to Baghdad. The Apaches remained with us even after we had dropped off our VIPs, making sure that our lone Blackhawk made it back to Balad – about 45 minutes' flying time away from the embassy – without incident. They didn't have to stay with us after we had dropped off our "cargo", but they did, and we were really grateful for their extra effort that day.'

This Lot 7 Apache from the 'Avengers' of A Company has just undergone a phased maintenance inspection and is conducting an engine run-up (*CW2 John Rawls*)

NEW PLUMAGE

One of the more interesting developments in the Apache community of late, and one that promises to catch on quickly, is a new experimental

This fire team from A company, 1-1 AVN was assigned as a special escort detail to the ambassador's UH-60 detachment from 171st AVN in late 2004 (*CW2 John Rawls*)

multiple grey paint scheme worn by the AH-64As of the 1st Battalion, 151st Aviation Regiment, known originally as the 'Marauders' – with the change in colour, the new call-sign 'Ghostrider' was adopted.

The South Carolina ARNG's 1-151st AVN received orders for deployment to Iraq in late 2003, and the unit began preparations at its McEntire Air National Guard Station base, in Eastover, just as any battalion would. It initially conducted a series of detailed maintenance checks of its 16-year-old AH-64As prior to readying them for shipment to Iraq in February 2004. Although this routine had been followed by all previous Apache outfits sent overseas as part of the War on Terror, 1-151st AVN had the distinction of being the first unit to field a new trial paint scheme for its helicopters.

Whilst its AH-64s were undergoing deep maintenance at MCAS Beaufort, South Carolina, they were repainted in an experimental, Marine-inspired, grey-blue uppersurfaces over light grey scheme in an attempt to better camouflage the aircraft during daylight operations. The light greys used by the Marines' AH-1Ws in Iraq had been particularly effective in daylight conditions, with helicopter crews in the air and soldiers on the ground routinely commenting on how difficult it was to spot the Super Cobras operating in-theatre.

Although the new scheme was applied directly over the Apaches' original 'Helo Olive Drab', which initially caused some weight and balance issues, the 'greys' have reportedly made the AH-64 just as difficult to spot during daylight operations as the appreciably smaller AH-1W, thus significantly enhancing the helicopter's survivability.

Commencing combat operations in the early summer of 2004, the 151st AVN was attached to Task Force *Olympia* in northern Iraq and began flying missions in support of the 1st Brigade ('Stryker'), 25th Infantry Division around Mosul. The battalion's tempo of combat operations increased dramatically in December 2004 following an influx

Seen here at Lake Docan in northern Iraq, this Apache provided the escort for British Foreign Secretary Jack Straw when he visited Iraq in the autumn of 2004 (*CW2 John Rawls*)

One of the more recent Apache developments has seen this South Carolina AH-64A (94-0332), along with the remaining 11 aircraft from A and B Companies of the 151st AVN, repainted in Marine greys before heading to Iraq. The new camouflage scheme is very effective in daylight operations (*William McCullough*)

A close-up of the tactical identifier
for the Palmetto battalion
(*William McCullough*)

A 'Ghostriders' Apache 'on the
wing', or should it be 'rotor'.
The effectiveness of the new
camouflage is readily apparent
in this photograph. Interestingly,
the battalion call-sign was originally
'Marauders', but after switching
to the grey paint scheme, it was
decided that 'Ghostrider' was
a more appropriate call-sign
(*US Army*)

of insurgents into the Mosul area in the wake of *Al Fajr*. A significant rise in the number of attacks on police stations, Coalition camps and convoys, as well as roadside bombings, have kept 151st AVN crews busy in the run up to the Iraqi general elections, scheduled for 30 January 2005.

The 151st suffered its first operational loss at 1930 hrs on 9 December when an AH-64 struck an idling UH-60 and exploded at the Mosul FARP whilst attempting to land in total darkness. Both Apache crewmen (CW4 Patrick D Leach and 1Lt Andrew C Shields) were killed and the four crewmembers of the Blackhawk injured, although the latter returned to duty within a few days.

Flying its distinctively camouflaged Apaches, the 151st has certainly made its presence felt within TF *Olympia*'s AO. Indeed, six of its aircrew recently earned their second combat patch nearly 40 years after receiving their first in Vietnam! One of these individuals was Apache pilot CW5 Jack Dalton, who flew Cobras in Vietnam with 3rd Sqn, 5th Cavalry. According to Dalton, 'We are today employing basically the same tactics as we did 35 years ago, with diving and running fire being the preferred attack plan. We also use the same type of rockets, just modernised.'

REORGANISATION

At its peak, the Apache strength in Iraq neared 150 helicopters. However, unit rotations, AH-64D conversion training and commitments elsewhere in the world have seen that number dwindle to no more than 50 aircraft, which are tasked with supporting ground units spread across the entire country. Company AOs have now been made much larger as a result so that fireteams can meet the greater demand placed on them for close combat support.

New Force Modernisation policies brought in since OIF have focused on the importance of the Apache to US forces tasked with fighting the War on Terror. In the new US Army Order of Battle, heavy US divisions will now have two AH-64 battalions assigned to them, while light divisions will each have a single battalion. This will allow two companies of Apaches to support a brigade combat team instead of just one, thus offering greater flexibility and far greater aerial firepower to the ground commander.

The implementation of the Force Modernisation has seen some Corps-level attack aviation units disbanded and reassigned to augment the active divisions. The first units to be reassigned were from the 229th Aviation Regiment, which was disbanded in the early summer of 2004. Its two active Apache battalions were symbolically deactivated and then reassigned to other units. The regiment's single reserve battalion will also be reassigned upon the completion of its tour in OIF III, which began in January 2005 with the unit supporting the New York ARNG's 42nd Infantry Division.

The 1st Battalion was redesignated 3rd Battalion, 3rd Aviation Regiment, supporting the 3rd Infantry Division, and it arrived in-theatre to participate in OIF III in January 2005. 3-3 AVN suffered an early fatality just days into its deployment when Capt Joe F Lusk was killed on 21 January at Camp Buehring, in Kuwait, whilst conducting an exercise prior to going into action in Iraq. His unidentified co-pilot/gunner was pulled from the wreckage of the AH-64D with serious injuries.

3-229th has also been reactivated as the 3rd Battalion, 82nd Aviation Regiment, where it will work in conjunction with the OH/AH-58 Kiowa Warriors of the1-82nd Attack. This reassignment returns the AH-64 to the 82nd Airborne Division, which was the unit that received the first Apaches to enter frontline service almost 15 years ago.

Similarly, the 11th Aviation Regiment will be disbanded, redesignating the 2-6th Cavalry as the 3-1st AVN for the 1st Infantry Division, and the 6-6th Cavalry will become the 3-501st AVN with the 1st Armored Division.

'Vietnam Inc'. Featured in the Stryker Brigade newsletter, these six gentlemen from the 151st AVN have earned their second combat patch in four decades, all having completed at least one tour in Vietnam over 30 years earlier. On the far left is CW5 Jack Dalton, who flew AH-1G Cobras in Vietnam, and who continues to fly gunships in Iraq as an Apache pilot with A Company, 151st AVN (*US Army*)

THE FUTURE

An Associated Press article on 4 August 2004 declared that, 'The Army is overhauling its helicopter corps after high-profile setbacks in Iraq. A battle lost, several crashes and the cancellation of the new Comanche stealth helicopter have led critics to suggest the aircraft is too fragile, vulnerable and ineffective for the modern battlefield.'

One only need look at the changes in the current Order of Battle to see that this is not the case. While certainly there have been some obstacles to overcome, the author of the previous statement fails to take into account the context under which those 'setbacks' occurred, and also fails to address the outstanding successes achieved by Apache units over the past two years of combat in two entirely separate, and vastly different, theatres of war. In the wake of OIF I, USAF generals began calling for the retirement of the Apache almost instantly. They believed that tactical jets armed with precision munitions such as JDAM and next generation LGBs could conduct close combat support better than an attack helicopter. However, in reality, the fact remains that when precise aerial ordnance delivery is needed close to friendly forces, troops on the ground will continue to call for Apache support for many years to come.

Indeed, the Boeing helicopter's future is looking bright, as its combat capabilities will be significantly increased with the introduction of the new Lot 8 AH-64D. This version features an upgraded communications suite, blue-force tracker systems and improved navigation aids. These new machines, which will see action in Iraq fairly soon, along with the deployment of the first US Army Longbow Apache units to Afghanistan, will continue to take the fight to the enemy.

APPENDICES

UNITS FLYING COMBAT MISSIONS IN OEF AND OIF

ACTIVE ARMY

1st Battalion, 1st Aviation Regiment, 1st Infantry Division, 'Gunfighters'
  A Company 'Taz Devils'
  B Company 'Wolfpack'
  C Company 'Ghostriders'

1st Battalion, 3rd Aviation Regiment, 3rd Infantry Division, 'Vipers'
  A Company 'Assassins'
  B Company 'Warlords'
  C Company 'Outcasts'

1st Battalion, 4th Aviation Regiment, 4th Infantry Division, 'Dragons'
  A Company 'Vipers'
  B Company 'Reapers'
  C Company 'Sidewinders'

1st Battalion, 101st Aviation Regiment, 101st Airborne Division, 'Expect No Mercy'
  A Company 'Spectres'
  B Company 'Bearcats'
  C Company 'Paladins'

2nd Battalion, 101st Aviation Regiment, 101st Airborne Division, 'Eagle Warrior'
  A Company 'Highlanders'
  B Company 'Gremlins'
  C Company 'Ghostriders'

3rd Battalion, 101st Aviation Regiment, 101st Airborne Division, 'Eagle Attack'
  A Company 'Killer Spades'
  B Company 'Blue Max'
  C Company 'Widowmakers'

1st Battalion, 227th Attack Helicopter Regiment, 1st Cavalry Division, 'First Attack'
  A Company 'Avengers'
  B Company 'Reapers'
  C Company 'Vampires'

1st Battalion, 229th Attack Helicopter Regiment, XVIII Airborne Corps, 'Tigersharks'
  A Company 'Stalkers'
  B Company 'Raiders'
  C Company 'Blue Max'

3rd Battalion, 229th Attack Helicopter Regiment, XVIII Airborne Corps, 'Flying Tigers'
  A Company 'Aces'
  B Company 'Predators'
  C Company 'Prowlers'

1st Battalion, 501st Aviation Regiment, 1st Armored Division, 'Dragons'
  A Company 'Assassins
  B Company 'Death Dealers'
  C Company 'Steel Hunters'

2nd Squadron, 6th Cavalry, 11th Attack Helicopter Regiment, 'Fighting Sixth'
  A Troop 'Blackjack'
  B Troop '
  C Troop

6th Squadron, 6th Cavalry, 11th Attack Helicopter Regiment, 'Six Shooters'
  A Troop 'Assassins'
  B Troop 'Pale Riders'
  C Troop 'Lighthorse'

4th Squadron, 3rd Armored Cavalry Regiment, 'Brave Rifles'
  R Troop 'Renegades'
  Q Troop 'Quicksilver'

ARMY NATIONAL GUARD

1st Battalion, 111th Aviation Regiment, Florida National Army Guard
  B Company 'Hog Hunters'

1st Battalion, 130th Aviation Regiment, North Carolina Army National Guard, 'Panthers'
  A Company
  B Company
  C Company

1st Battalion, 151st Aviation Regiment, South Carolina Army National Guard, 'Ghostriders'
  A Company 'Nightmare'
  B Company 'Mustang'

1st Battalion, 211th Aviation Regiment, Utah Army National Guard
  B Company 'Buccaneers'

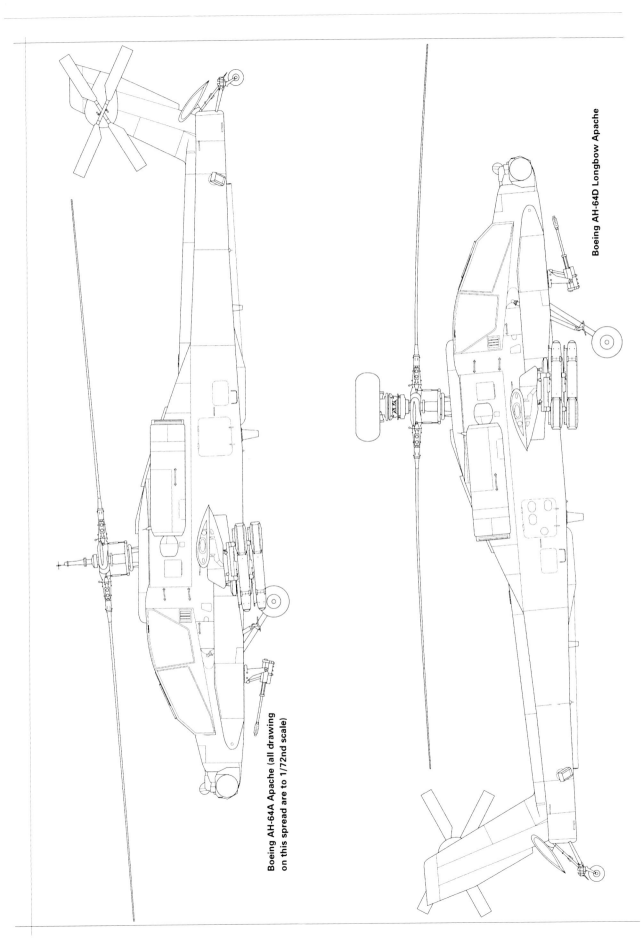

Boeing AH-64A Apache (all drawing
on this spread are to 1/72nd scale)

Boeing AH-64D Longbow Apache

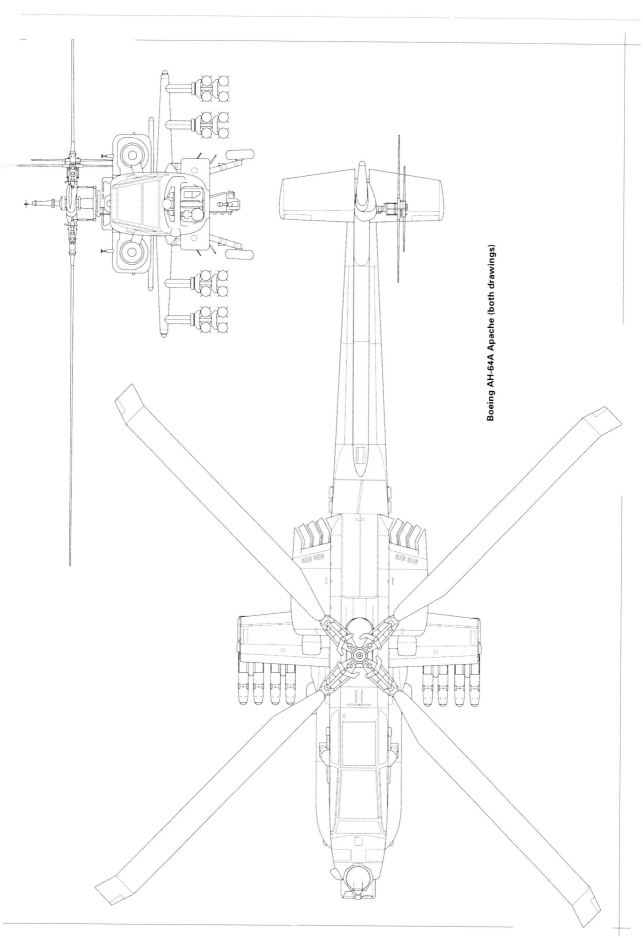

Boeing AH-64A Apache (both drawings)

COLOUR PLATES

1

AH-64A 88-0209 of A Company, 3-101 ATKHB, 101st Airborne Division, Bagram, Afghanistan, March 2002

Amongst the first AH-64s to arrive in Afghanistan in January 2002, this Apache was one of seven engaged on D-Day of Operation *Anaconda* (2 March 2002) in the Shah-i-Kot valley. It is armed with two 19-shot M261 rocket pods and two four-shot Hellfire racks, each with two AGM-114K Hellfire II missiles. This aircraft was destroyed in a crash on 11 April 2002, the Apache coming down due to mechanical failure.

2

AH-64A 90-0288 of A Company, 3-101 ATKHB, 101st Airborne Division, Bagram, Afghanistan, March 2002

Another Operation *Anaconda* participant, this AH-64A flew with the 3rd Battalion throughout the brigade's tenure in Afghanistan. The airframe was damaged on several occasions, but was repaired and continued flying combat missions until the 3rd Brigade, 101st Airborne returned to the US in June 2002. It is still currently serving with the unit, based at Fort Campbell/Campbell Army Air Field, Kentucky.

3

AH-64A 89-0245 *DELIVERANCE* of B Company, 1-229 ATKHB, XVIII Airborne Corps, Bagram, Afghanistan, November 2002

Flown by CW3 Zac Noble throughout the 1-229th's tour in Afghanistan, this Apache flew over 500 combat hours during the battalion's tour, and took numerous AAA hits throughout. On one particular mission, *DELIVERANCE* was struck by small-arms fire in the transmission, losing all its oil and forcing the crew to hastily disengage. Able to land out of harm's way and refill the oil reservoir, CW3 Noble and 1Lt Steve Bouchard nursed the stricken helicopter safely back to base. When they landed 90 minutes later, the transmission was totally dry. This aircraft is still serving with 1-229 ATKHB at Fort Bragg/Simmons Army Air Field, North Carolina.

4

AH-64A 88-0202 *DEVIL'S DANCE* of C Company, 1-229 ATKHB, XVIII Airborne Corps, Kandahar, Afghanistan, autumn 2002

This AH-64A went through several variations of markings during its time in Afghanistan. Initially, its name *DEVIL'S DANCE* (inspired by heavy metal band Metallica's song of the same name) appeared in white ahead of the upper laser detector, although this was later painted black. At some point in the latter stages of the deployment, the Maltese Cross of the 'Blue Max' was added to the aft end of the engine nacelles. The helicopter's

black 'sharksmouth' was standard for all 'Tigersharks' AH-64s, since the entire 229th Attack Helicopter Regiment can trace its lineage to the American Volunteer Group 'Flying Tigers' of World War 2 fame. *DEVIL'S DANCE* is armed with two four-shot Hellfire missile racks, each carrying a single AGM-114K Hellfire II, and two 19-shot M261 rocket pods, containing four Flechette (which are longer, since they house 1200 steel darts) and 15 HE rounds. This weapons fit, along with a 130-gallon belly tank in place of the 30 mm ammunition tray, soon became the norm in OEF. While losing the ammunition tray eliminated 1110 rounds for the cannon (90 rounds could be carried in the feed chute), it allowed the 'Blue Max' Apache crews to markedly increase their mission time, and therefore offer greater support to Coalition troops on the ground. 88-0202 is presently the oldest Apache serving with 1-229 ATKHB at Fort Bragg/Simmons Army Air Field.

5

AH-64A 89-0260 *DAMAGE INC.* of C Company, 3-229 ATKHB, XVIII Airborne Corps, Kandahar, Afghanistan, early 2003

When the 1-229th ATKHB left Afghanistan in early 2003, it turned its Apaches over to sister battalion 3-229 ATKHB. The 21 helicopters continued flying with the new battalion throughout its deployment, while the 1-229th returned to Fort Hood, Texas, to transition to the AH-64D. *DAMAGE INC.* (also named for a Metallica song) was flown by C Company on numerous counterinsurgency and close combat attack missions in 2003. Its markings, and the armament it carries, are very similar to those seen on both *DELIVERANCE* and *DEVIL'S DANCE*, although the 'Blue Max' on the aft end of the nacelle has been painted over.

6

AH-64D 99-5102 of B Company, 1-3 ATKHB, 3rd Infantry Division, southern Iraq, 20 March 2003

As in Operation *Desert Storm*, the AH-64 fired the first shots of Operation *Iraqi Freedom* when this aircraft from the 'Warlords' of the 3rd Aviation Regiment launched its Hellfire missiles at several Iraqi observation posts on the Iraq–Kuwait border ahead of the advancing 3rd Infantry Division. Adorned with the 'Vipers'' ubiquitous white 'sharksmouth' (all 18 AH-64Ds assigned to 1-3 ATKHB featured 'teeth') inspired by the markings worn on the unit's AH-1Gs in Vietnam, this aircraft also boasts APG-78 mast-mounted fire control radar (FCR). Half of the battalion's Apaches were fitted with FCR, the 'Vipers' using the aircraft to scan the battlefield for targets. The crews of these machines then relayed digital targeting information to non-FCR-equipped AH-64Ds. All 1-3 ATKHB aircraft were identically armed during the early stages of OIF, employing the 30 mm cannon,

2.75-in rockets – either high explosive (HE), multi-purpose submunition (MPSM) or Flechette rounds – and both Radar-Frequency (RF) and Semi-Active Laser (SAL) Hellfire III missiles. A typical load for an OIF mission was eight Hellfire IIIs (four on each inboard pylon), with one RF and three SAL missiles being carried per side. Nineteen-shot M261 rocket pods, featuring a combination of HE, MPSM or Flechette, were carried on the outer pylons. 99-5102 currently remains a part of 1-3 ATKHB at Fort Stewart/Hunter Army Air Field, Georgia.

7

AH-64D 99-5118 of C Company, 1-3 ATKHB, 3rd Infantry Division, An Nasiriyah, Iraq, 31 March 2003

Also the subject of the cover artwork for this volume, 'Outcasts' AH-64D 99-5118, piloted by CW3 Rob Purdy and CW2 Nick DiMona, flew an urgent medevac escort mission on 31 March 2003. Having just returned from a combat sortie, Purdy and DiMona were shutting down their Apache when their relief took off in 99-5104, lost visibility in the swirling sand and crashed. Purdy and DiMona ran to the wrecked Apache and pulled its shaken, but relatively unharmed crew, to safety. The two then returned to their aircraft and took off, escorting the 3rd ID medevac UH-60 to Nasiriyah. Five wounded (three Americans and two Iraqis) were duly recovered and brought to safety. As with all 1-3 AH-64Ds, the 'sharksmouth' is painted in white on the forward portion of the avionics sponson. The eye, located ahead of the co-pilot/gunner's window, is white, with a red pupil. This particular machine's starboard wing stub is carrying a Hellfire rack inboard and a single M261 rocket pod outboard.

8

AH-64D 98-5061 of 1-101 ATKHB, 101st Airborne Division, Mosul, Iraq, late April 2003

Seen in Mosul after major combat was declared over, this AH-64D entered combat with the 1st Battalion in late March, clearing areas ahead of the division through Najaf and Karbala. The division's three Apache battalions provided a screening force ahead of the advancing elements, conducting deep-attack missions along with forward reconnaissance and close support sorties.

9

AH-64D 97-5032 of A Company, 2-101 ATKHB, 101st Airborne Division, Mosul, Iraq, summer 2003

Launched on the crucially important Apache deep-attack mission of 28 March 2003, 97-5032 helped the 2-101st successfully accomplish its mission by eliminating numerous Iraqi tanks and vehicles. However, upon returning to FOB 'Shell' after the sortie, the crew of the A Company machine got into zero-visibility conditions due to the swirling sand while attempting to land. Losing any reference point by which to set the helicopter down, the crew landed hard, inflicting Class A

damage on the machine when it rolled over. Subsequently repaired, 97-5032 is presently the oldest Apache serving with 2-101 AVN at Campbell Army Air Field.

10

AH-64D 99-5135 of C Company, 1-227 ATKHB, 1st Cavalry Division, OPCONNed to 11th Aviation Regiment (Attack), Karbala, Iraq, 24 March 2003

This AH-64D was one of 31 sent on a deep-attack mission to hit elements of the Republican Guard Medina Division in and around the city of Karbala. The 11th Aviation Regiment ran headlong into the most concentrated and well-coordinated anti-aircraft fire encountered during the initial phases of combat. Both this machine and an Apache from 6-6 Cavalry were badly hit by ground fire, although the 'Six Shooters' helicopter was able to limp home on one engine. However, 99-5135, flown by CW2s Ronald Young and David Williams, suffered a hard landing in a field near Karbala, where its crew was pinned down by enemy fire and eventually captured by Iraqi soldiers. Even though the 1-227th was OPCONNed to the 11th Aviation Regiment, this machine clearly shows its affiliation with its parent division with the crossed sabres and 1st Cavalry Division marking worn on the forward section of its avionics sponson. The C Company identifier – a vampire bat – is visible on the tail in black, outlined in white, above the serial number. Within hours of the Apache having come down, US Army artillery forces used a barrage from a Multiple Launch Rocket System to destroy the helicopter.

11

AH-64D 00-5220 of B Troop, 6-6th Cavalry, 11th Aviation Regiment (Attack), Karbala, Iraq, 24 March 2003

One of the 13 AH-64Ds fielded by the 6-6th Cavalry on the night of 23 March to strike the Medina Division in Karbala, this Apache received numerous small-arms hits during the intense firefight. CW4 Bob Duffney and CW2 Bill Neal crewed the aircraft, which was the lead Apache in B Troop during the mission. When 'all hell broke loose' and everyone started taking fire, Duffney and Neal remained on station over the city, engaging ground targets. The last crew from B Troop to egress, Duffney and Neal made sure that their wingmen, CW2 Mike Tomblin and 1Lt Jason King, made it to safety after the latter was hit by a rifle round in the throat. Both helicopters landed in the desert west of Najaf, where the crew assessed 1Lt King's injuries and got him back to an aid station for treatment to his non-life-threatening wound. King returned to flight status with 6-6th Cavalry in Iraq a week later following minor surgery. The 'Pale Rider' symbol adorning the helicopter's outboard rocket pods was the unit's only identifier in OIF, the marking consisting of a white, mounted figure in silhouette wielding a battleaxe, patterned after a fantasy character created by artist Boris Vallejo.

12
AH-64D 00-5211 of A Troop, 6-6th Cavalry, 11th Aviation Regiment (Attack), Karbala, Iraq, 24 March 2003
AH-64D 00-5211 was also a participant in the ill-fated 23 March mission to Karbala, being flown on this occasion by Capt Stephen Murphy and CW3 Martin Kaltwang. The Apache bears the tactical identifiers of A Troop – a Stetson-adorned skull of the 'Assassins' – on the outboard rocket pod. Also of note are the red/white cavalry nameplates on both the pilot and co-pilot/gunner's doors, identifying the helicopter's assigned crew. A similar marking could be found on the port side in the pilot's window, which identified the aircraft's crew chief as Sgt Anthony Gadson. This aircraft crash-landed near Balad on 30 October 2003 following an in-flight engine fire that started in the APU. Both crewmen succeeded in escaping the blaze without injury, but the Apache was completely burned out.

13
AH-64A 86-8955 of A Troop, 2-6th Cavalry, 11th Aviation Regiment (Attack), Objective *Talon*, Iraq, April 2003
One of the oldest AH-64As to participate in OIF, 86-8955 was a veteran of combat in *Desert Storm* in 1991 and the policing operation in Bosnia in 1995-96 (the latter with 227th AVN) – note the '0' prefixing its serial on the tail, which denotes that this particular airframe is more than ten years old. Although 2-6th Cavalry missed out on the 23 March Karbala raid, it was soon thrust into action during the final assault on Baghdad. Flown primarily by CW4 Greg Inman and Capt Joel Magsig (call-sign 'Blackjack 6'), the Apache flew in support of the 3rd Infantry Division's taking of Baghdad on 2–4 April. It also became the first American aircraft to land at BIAP on 4 April after it had been damaged while escorting a 3rd ID medevac UH-60. Engaged by an armed SUV hiding in a grove of trees, the helicopter had its fire control system damaged, forcing the crew to land at the nearest airfield – BIAP! The 'Blackjack' Troop tactical identifier (a large white triangle containing a white '7') is stencilled on the aft end of the engine nacelle.

14
AH-64D 01-5241 of C Company, 1-4th ATKHB, 4th Infantry Division, Tikrit, Iraq, autumn 2003
Although the 4th Infantry Division arrived in Iraq right at the end of major hostilities, the 'Dragons' of 1-4th AVN saw considerable combat during their year in Iraq. This C Company aircraft, flown as 'Sidewinder 06' by Capt John Tucker and CW3 Baker, was heavily involved in supporting counterinsurgency operations during the unit's tenure at FOB 'Speicher'.

15
AH-64A 87-0425 of B Company, 1-501st ATKHB, 1st Armored Division, Balad, Iraq, January 2004
One of the more garishly marked AH-64s to see combat in Iraq, this 'Death Dealers' Apache displays a full 'sharksmouth' reminiscent of the marking which adorns A-10s of the USAF's 23rd Fighter Wing. A white eye, with a red pupil, is carried below the co-pilot/gunner's window. A white stencilled square, framing a three-inch white '25', adorns the aft end of the engine nacelle. Primarily tasked with performing convoy escort, reconnaissance and aerial security, 501st Apaches provided attack aviation support for the entire 1st Armored Division during OIF II. This aircraft had previously served with the 1st Battalion, 111th Aviation Regiment, Florida Army National Guard, prior to being transferred to the 1-501st ATKHB at Hanau Army Air Field, Germany, in late 2003.

16
AH-64A 88-0197 of C Company, 1-501st ATKHB, 1st Armored Division, Baghdad, Iraq, December 2003
This machine was the first Lot 7 AH-64A to enter service with the US Army in early 1989. Bearing the C Company tactical identifier on its engine nacelle (a white stenciled circle, which here contains the number 97), this machine flew missions with C Company throughout its time in Iraq, providing aerial support to the ground brigades of the 1st Armored Division.

17
AH-64A 87-0428 of A Company, 1-1st ATKHB, 1st Infantry Division, Irbil, Iraq, October 2004
The 1st Infantry Division deployed to Iraq in the spring of 2004, bringing with it the 1st Battalion, 1st Aviation, known as the 'Gunfighters'. The 'Taz Devils' of A Company were stationed at Irbil, in northern Iraq, upon the unit's arrival in-theatre. Its Apaches all had a cartoon Tasmanian Devil stencilled on the forward ends of their avionics bays, with the last two digits of the aircraft's serial emblazoned on the creature's belly. 'Taz 28' is seen here as it appeared on the Irbil flightline in October 2004.

18
AH-64A 87-0474 of B Company, 1-1st ATKHB, 1st Infantry Division, FOB 'Speicher', Iraq, December 2004
This Apache was flown by CW2s Mylon Gladden and Micah Johnson on a VIP escort mission conducted on 31 December 2004. The two-aircraft Apache team (87-0474 and 87-0417) escorted two UH-60s from B Company, 171st AVN to Camp 'Echo', in northern Iraq. Unlike the 'Taz Devils', the 'Wolfpack' of B Company have not applied any distinctive insignia other than the white squares stencilled onto the aft end of their engine nacelles. This marking is also occasionally seen on the outboard rocket pods.

19
AH-64D 02-5296 of A Company, 1-227th ATKHB, 1st Cavalry Division, Balad, Iraq, November 2004
The 1st Battalion, 227th Attack Helicopter

Regiment was the first Apache unit to return to Iraq for a second tour, this time serving with its parent division, the 1st Cavalry. The 1-227th, based at Balad, to the north-west of Baghdad, flew numerous combat sorties in the 'Sunni Triangle' in 2004–05. The AH-64Ds of 'Avenger' Company all had the eagle head (with a superimposed American flag) stencilled on the tail, while an A Company tactical identifier (a small blue triangle) is visible at the aft end of the Apache's M261 rocket pod. This particular AH-64, which does not have its APG-78 radar fitted, is one of the newest Apaches to have seen service in Iraq to date, having only been delivered to the Army by Boeing in March 2003.

20
AH-64A 87-0453 of 1-130th ATKHB, North Carolina Army National Guard, Kandahar, Afghanistan, January 2004
The first Army National Guard attack helicopter battalion committed to combat operations in the Global War on Terror, the 1-130th ATKHB deployed to Afghanistan in the autumn of 2003. The central element of Task Force *Panther*, the 130th led a mixed, brigade-sized unit comprised of Active Duty and ARNG units, as well as active and reserve Marine Corps assets, in support of 10th Mountain Division combat operations in eastern Afghanistan. As with all 1-130th AH-64As, a Black Panther motif dominates the aft end of the engine nacelle. This veteran machine (which was delivered to the Army in early 1988) had previously served with the 2-6th Cavalry in Germany, but had been passed on to the ARNG when the unit converted to AH-64Ds upon its move to Camp Humphreys/Desiderio Army Air Field in Pyongtaek, South Korea, in the autumn of 2003.

21
AH-64A 94-0332 of 1-151st ATKHB, South Carolina Army National Guard, Mosul, Iraq, December 2004
Hastily repainted before the unit deployed in the late spring of 2004, the 1-151st's AH-64As were the first Army Apaches to wear an experimental two-grey paint scheme inspired by the Marine Corps' AH-1Ws in OIF. In order to get access to the correct shades of paint for the scheme, the unit's Apaches were resprayed at MCAS Cherry Point, North Carolina. The two-tone scheme comprised grey-blue (FS 35414) uppersurfaces and light grey (FS 35526) fuselage sides and undersurfaces. It will be interesting to see how this experimental paint scheme evolves in coming years. This particular aircraft (94-0332) was amongst the last batch of ten AH-64As built for the US Army, making it practically a brand new aircraft in relation to some of the other 'warhorses' featured in this colour section. Unlike its older cousins, this helicopter also carries the new AH-64D-style national markings and tail number.

Back cover
AH-64A 91-0114 of B Company, 1-211th ATKHB, Utah Army National Guard, FOB 'Orgun-E', Afghanistan, December 2004
One of the very few AH-64As to carry nose art other than a name or 'sharksmouth', this Apache has a rocket-carrying yellow jacket (a type of hornet) painted on its right avionics bay. Crew names are blocked in black by each access door, and the names themselves are written in yellow. Still in-country when this volume went to press, the 211th, along with B Company, 111th AVN, have continued flying anti-insurgent patrols from the Army's facility at Kandahar air base against Taleban and al-Qaeda fighters, as well as the forces of warlord Gulbuddin Hekmatyar throughout OEF IV.

INDEX